THE
UNITED STATES ARMY
MARKSMANSHIP UNIT

PISTOL MARKSMANSHIP

GUIDE

Fredonia Books
Amsterdam, The Netherlands

Pistol Marksmanship Guide

by
United States Army Marksmanship Unit

ISBN: 1-58963-631-7

Reprinted from the 1980 edition

Fredonia Books
Amsterdam, the Netherlands
http://www.fredoniabooks.com

FOREWORD

The United States Army Marksmanship Unit has compiled this guide with the intent of providing assistance to pistol marksmen throughout the United States. Much of the information has been contributed by championship caliber U.S. Army pistol shooters and coaches. The text is designed for ready reference and contains the fundamentals of pistol marksmanship and the most advanced techniques known to these experts. The data presented represents a comprehensive coverage of the many facets of pistol marksmanship and related subjects. Portions of the information contained herein were obtained from the research of authoritative articles, personal interviews and observation of foreign competitions. Noteworthy contributions were received from many experienced persons closely associated with pistol activities not connected with military training.

This guide is dedicated to the individual marksman who is seriously interested in improving his performance in the art of pistol competition.

This publication was prepared in compliance with that portion of the mission of the United States Army Marksmanship Unit which requires the continuing improvement of training methods and techniques so as to raise the standards of pistol marksmanship skill in the United States Army.

The information published in this book is not for sale and/or resale for commercial purposes but is intended for furthering the aims and objectives of the civilian/military marksmanship programs being conducted in the United States.

Suggestions, criticism, or comments that will contribute to attaining these objectives are solicited and may be directed to the Commanding Officer, USAMU, Fort Benning, Georgia 31905.

STANLEY J. PARMENTIER
Colonel, Infantry
Commanding

i

THE PISTOL MARKSMANSHIP MANUAL

TABLE OF CONTENTS

SECTION ONE

FUNDAMENTALS OF PISTOL MARKSMANSHIP

The fundamentals of pistol marksmanship embrace all of those physical factors essential to the firing of an accurate shot. Accuracy, in this sense, assumes that the weapon is zeroed, that a high degree of inherent accuracy exists in both the weapon and the ammunition, and that the firing is taking place under ideal conditions.

Essentially, accurate shooting with a pistol requires no elements other than those described in the following sentence: ALIGN THE SIGHTS PROPERLY ON THAT PART OF THE TARGET REQUIRED FOR YOUR GROUP TO CENTER IN THE TARGET AREA AND CAUSE THE HAMMER TO FALL WITH-OUT DISTURBING THAT ALIGNMENT. All elements of pistol shooting such as position, grip, sight alignment, breathe control, trigger control, physical condition, and psychology of shooting, when perfected, simply enables the shooter to perform the action described in the above key sentence.

In order for a shot to be accurate, it is first necessary to make sure that the pistol will be held as motionless as it is possible to do so during the time that the shot is being fired. The stance assumed by the shooter must provide the greatest stability possible for both the shooter's body and the weapon.

To obtain a minimum arc of movement the shooter must give the pistol a definite stability of direction. Proper body position points the pistol directly toward the target with no tendency to drift or move to either side. Likewise, the vertical movement of the pistol is confined to the aiming area. Breathing is accompanied by the rhythmic movement of the chest, and in order to keep the pistol as immobile as possible, the shooter must hold his breath for the length of time required to deliver an accurate shot. To obtain correct sight alignment, it is necessary for the shooter to grip the pistol in a manner which guarantees that he is holding the pistol firmly and that trigger pressure is applied straight to the rear. The delicate balance of sight alignment and minimum arc of movement can be easily disturbed if the trigger is activated in a manner which causes excess movement. However, since the shooter cannot achieve complete immobility when assuming the stance and position, the trigger has to be pressed during some movement of the pistol. In order to deliver an accurate shot within his ability to hold, the shooter must not only press the trigger evenly, but he must do so with correct sight alignment. The size of the shot group will, therefore, not exceed the dimensions of the arc of movement, provided the shot breaks as a surprise and no reflex action of muscles disturbs the delivery of the shot.

To help the shooter acquire the necessary knowledge to master all the factors that control his shooting, we shall analyze in detail each separate element of accurate shooting - stance, position, grip, holding the breath, sight alignment, and control of the trigger. Also included will be certain methods of training that will accelerate the shooter's development into a champion pistol shot. This status is achieved only after the shooter has mastered the technique of executing the fundamentals.

CHAPTER I

ATTAINING A MINIMUM ARC OF MOVEMENT

It is necessary during firing to press the trigger under varying conditions of pistol movement in conjunction with correct sight alignment. In order to apply coordinated pressure on the trigger, the shooter must wait for those very definite times when all control factors are optimum and firing conditions become favorable. The rule that must be observed as the first step in attaining control of your shooting is: "You must never attempt to fire until you have completely settled into a minimum arc of movement."

In order to learn how to fire a shot at the proper time, the shooter must make analysis of the time needed to settle and the duration of the minimum arc of movement.

The entire system, consisting of the shooter's body and the pistol, always undergoes a degree of movement. This is sometimes a pulsating, swaying or erratic arc of movement during aiming and firing a shot. The cause of this movement aside from conditions such as weather, is the action of the muscles maintaining the shooter's body in a definite position. Other action such as blood pulsation, causes movement of individual parts of the shooter's body and the pistol. The nature and extent of the arc of movement changes within the time being devoted to delivering a shot. For example, when the shooter is first getting his sight alignment and has not yet had time to settle his body and pistol, the extent of the movement is relatively great. As the body becomes balanced and the aiming is more precise, the arc of movement minimizes. After a certain length of time, the minimum arc of movement begins to increase, because the muscles begin to fatigue, and the shooter does not have enough air in his lungs to continue holding his breath. If we record the arc of movement, we will see a wavelike line with varying amplitude of oscillations (Figure 1-1).

Figure 1-1. Basic Scheme of Minimum Arc of Movement.

It is obvious that under such circumstances the shooter must begin his smooth pressure on the trigger while not devoting too much attention to the arc of movement as long as it remains at the minimum. Continue to apply pressure on the trigger and intensely concentrate on keeping the sights in alignment. The resulting five to seven second period is the most favorable time for firing an accurate shot.

Taking into consideration the direct relationship between accuracy of shooting and the degree of immobility of the pistol when the shot is being delivered, the marksman must give greatest consideration to the selection of a stance, a position, a grip, and a means of breath control which will guarantee the greatest stability to both the pistol and the body. The relatively small degree of movement thus obtained provides a stable foundation, permitting use of the other fundamentals.

A. THE STANCE.

The excellence of the stance is a major factor in creating conditions for maximum control. A high degree of control is necessary for the delivery of an accurate shot. Every individual possesses a combination of individual characteristics that are peculiar to him alone. Among these are height, weight, proportion of body, development of muscle system, etc. It follows, then, that there cannot be any definite, all-purpose stance which applies equally to all shooters. Therefore, the shooter himself, on the basis of his own particular configurations, must find the variation of stance which provides the greatest degree of stability for his body.

1. <u>The Main Requirements of the Stance</u>: The assumed stance is the position of the human body to support a pistol aimed at a target. Despite the great number of physical differences encountered in any cross-section of shooters, the stance must provide for:

a. The greatest possible degree of equilibrium and stability in the body-weapon system with the least possible strain on the shooter's muscles.

b. A head position which will allow for the most efficient use of the shooter's eyes throughout the sighting and aiming process.

Throughout the process of training it is necessary, therefore, for the shooter to exercise special care in the selection of a stance. The development of a poor stance should be detected and corrected early in the training program. Otherwise, it may require the breaking of deeply ingrained habits later.

Considering the role played by the muscles, bones and ligaments in the creation of stability in the shooter's stance, it is necessary for the shooter to understand the makeup of the human body. See Section Five, Annex I for supplemental information entitled, "Charaeteristics of the Human Body Relevant to Stance, Position and Grip."

2. <u>Assuming the stance:</u>

a. When assuming the firing stance, the head must be held as level as possible, so that the shooter can see the target directly in line with the arm and sights. It is necessary to take all steps to eliminate the tilting of the head to the right or left or an excessive tilting forward. It is not necessary to look **sideways** or to look at the sights from beneath the eyebrows. The head should not be pushed forward closer to the rear sight; neither should the head be tilted back excessively. This causes undue tension upon the neck muscles and, as a consequence, a slight movement of the head develops from fatigue. This may hinder the maintenance of perfect sight alignment.

b. When assuming a firing stance, the shooter must support the extended arm holding a weapon. As a result, the muscular system undergoes considerable strain. It must not only maintain the shooter's body in a definite position but must also exert a counteraction to the rather large weight of the suspended gun.

c. A shooter supporting a weapon constitutes a single system with a common center of gravity (Figure 1-2). Since the entire system is in equilibrium only when its line of gravity runs through the support area, (Figure 1-3), the holding of the weapon causes a change in the relative position of the individual parts of the body. A compensating displacement is brought about by the necessity to create a counteraction to the weight of the pistol and supporting arm. This compensating displacement of the parts of the body changes the shooter's posture. As a result, when he assumes a firing stance, his body takes on an asymmetric position which is unnatural. The preservation of the body's equilibrium in this unnatural posture requires that a greater load be placed upon the muscles and ligaments reinforcing the movable portions of the body.

d. The shooter has the task of finding for himself a suitable stance which will achieve immobility of the body without an excessive strain on muscles.

Let us assume that the shooter takes a stance for firing that will preserve the natural, erect posture of the body. He will strive to keep it erect with small compensating deviations of the muscle system. Thus, the extended arm holding a pistol places great tension on the muscles in the back and shoulders. In addition, if the shooter's figure is examined from the side, it will become obvious that when the shooter's body is kept stiffly erect, the body will be slightly unstable. The keeping of the body rigid will result in early fatigue and cause undesirable movement.

e. What posture should be given to the body in order to best support the weapon with the least expenditure of muscular effort?

3

Figure 1-2. Situation of the Over-all Center of Gravity of the Entire System
Consisting of the Shooter's Body and Weapon.

The shooter must hold his body in something less than an erect posture, with a slight rearward
bend in the back and the pelvis brought slightly forward. In this posture, the body has the vertical
line of the center of gravity shifted back of the axis of the hip joints. In such a pose, the body is kept
stable in the hip joints not so much by the work of the muscles, but by strong ligaments. The relaxed
immobility of the body is attained by counterbalancing the weight of the upper body against the extended
firing arm and pistol, and transfer much of the weight to the spinal column.

      f. The selection of the most stable stance will include giving the body a certain degree of
bend. As shown by practice, the shooter has nothing to fear in giving his body an asymmetric pose.

      g. The stability of the firing arm and weapon depends to an extent upon the correct place-
ment of the feet. This determines the support area for the shooter's body. The most stable and most
comfortable stance will be when the feet create a support area in the shape of a trapezoid with the
feet placed apart, approximately shoulder width. The toes should be spread apart slightly (Figure 1-3).
This placement of the feet creates not only a comparatively large support area, but is also the most
favorable positioning of the feet for avoiding muscular strain in the legs.

Figure 1-3. Placement of the Body's Support Surfaces - Both Feet - in Relation
to One Another, Creating the Support Area for Firing.

4

h. When assuming the firing stance, the shooter should not attempt to bring the legs too close to one another. Narrow placement of the legs decreases the support area and will result in a loss of stability, causing movement of the firing arm along the horizontal. Do not place the legs too far apart, as this creates undesirable strain on the inner arches of the feet, straining the leg muscles and holding the hip joints rigid, which leads to fatigue and an increase in the arc of movement.

i. In order for the stance to be a stable one, the shooter must, first, distribute the weight of his body, the arm and pistol evenly on both legs; second, the load placed on each leg must pass through the middle of the foot or close to the balls of the feet. When the weight of the body is distributed in this way the body's line of gravity will run through the middle of the support area. The stance will be the most stable when the muscles of both legs carry the same load. The coordinated work of these leg muscles results in the body's weight being alternately shifted in slight corrective moves in order to maintain balance.

j. The degree of strain upon the muscles and ligaments of the knee joints is of importance in the stability of the stance. The insufficiently rigid position of the knee joints will lead to an increase in the body's movement as a whole. By holding one leg straight and keeping the other one partially bent, varying tensions will exert excessive tension on the leg muscles. Inflexible straightening of the legs also causes tension of the leg muscles which leads to a loss of stability.

k. The group of muscles which do not directly participate in maintaining the shooter's body in the vertical position or holding the pistol aimed at the target is the muscles of the left arm and hand, the left-hand portion of the chest, the neck muscles, the abdomen, and the buttocks, must be relaxed as much as possible.

It is necessary to properly position the left or free arm and hand (for right-handed shooter). The free hand should be inserted into the left side pocket in a relaxed manner, or you may hook the left thumb over the waist belt. In relaxation of the left arm and shoulder, the free arm must not be allowed to hang loose, as any wind or recoiling of the body during firing will cause the free arm to swing, transferring to the body any movement.

l. The pistol arm should be extended with the wrist stiff and the elbow locked without strain. The arm must be straight, firmly extended and with no unnecessary tension of the muscles. This establishes solid arm control.

m. The body weight center of gravity should be brought forward slightly from the center of the support area, with a very slight shift toward the tips of the feet to reduce the action of the balance correcting mechanism. This is apparent in the alternate tensing and relaxing of the muscles of the legs, abdomen and lower back. This action to regain equilibrium is continuous. The body cannot remain motionless because the equilibrium does not remain constant. The constant corrective process causes an almost imperceptible weaving or sway.

3. The stance factor is so essential that a step-by-step summary of all of the points important to a proper stance is in order.

a. Stance must provide for:

(1) The greatest possible degree of equilibrium and stability of the shooter's body and weapon with the least possible strain on the shooter's muscular system, and the smallest movement possible of any part of the body, the shooting arm and the pistol.

(2) A head position which will allow for the most favorable conditions for the operation of the eyes during aiming.

b. During training, the shooter must take special care that he is not developing an incorrect stance or body posture which will require a breaking of habits later.

c. The shooter should become familiar with assuming the proper stance and practice getting the same stance each time it is assumed. The requirements are:

(1) The feet are separated about the width of the shoulders or slightly less, toes pointed out slightly.

5

Figure 1-4.

(2) Stand up erect and relaxed.

(3) The legs should be straight, but not stiff, knees firmly straight but not rigidly locked.

(4) The hips should be level and in a natural position.

(5) The abdomen should be relaxed.

(6) The shoulders and head should be level. No humping over or slouching with an unnatural tilt to the head.

(7) The non-shooting arm should be relaxed, the free hand in the side pocket or thumb hooked over the belt, not hanging loose.

(8) The pistol arm should be extended with the wrist stiff and the elbow locked without strain.

(9) The body weight center of gravity should be brought forward slightly from the center of the support area, with a very slight shift toward the tips of the feet to reduce the action of the balance correcting mechanism.

B. POSITION.

When preparing for accurate shooting, it is insufficient merely to assume a comfortable and stable stance. You must be able to aim or point at your target in a natural, consistent manner. Improper position will affect your ability to establish or maintain the hold in the center of the aiming area. Before each shot or string of shots, it is necessary to check the correctness of the assumed position with respect to the target. Avoid unnecessary muscular tension in the effort to hold in the aiming area. An adverse effect upon the movement of the shooting arm and weapon is caused by extra muscular effort.

Match competition requires the shooter to fire a large number of shots in one day. It is necessary to find the most effective position, which will allow the shooter's body to assume an identical position over a long period of time without causing undue strain upon the muscular system. Any feeling of discomfort, fatigue, constraint or a continuing necessity to correct the orientation of the body to the target distracts the shooter's attention from the principal goal; the uniform, absolute control of an accurate shot. The finding of the most effective position when firing will provide for a consistent pointing of the shooting arm and weapon and provide a free and unforced feeling of natural alignment with the target during the entire period of shooting.

1. The shooter must position himself so as to naturally align or point himself and his weapon with the target so the hold will remain in the desired area without a tendency of the shooting arm to drift away from the aiming area.

2. To orient or align yourself properly with the target, use the following method:

a. First face approximately 40 to 50 degrees from the target using the methods of assuming the stance previously mentioned.

b. Look at the target by turning only the head. Keep the head level and turn it far enough toward the target to allow the eyes to look straight out of the head.

c. Raise the arm to align with the target. Close your eyes, raise your pistol arm a foot or two above the horizontal and then allow it to settle back relaxed and naturally to the horizontal. Completely relax the arm and shoulder not being used. Repeat this procedure once or twice and settle into a natural point. A true, natural point is not obtained with the eyes open.

d. After settling into a natural point, open your eyes to check if your arm and pistol are aligned with the target. If the pistol has settled in the center of the target, you have your natural position.

Figure 1-5. Getting the Grip.

8

Figure 1-6. The Grip.

e. If the arm settles to one side of the target center, move your rear foot in the direction of error. Maintain without change the stance of the body as a unit from the feet to the shoulders and head. Swing the whole body by shifting the position of the feet until the arm and pistol are naturally aligned on the center of the target. Tests such as this will readily indicate your natural position. In no instance must the shooter correct errors in hold by moving the arm independent of the body. This type of correction is purely artificial and the arm will revert to the original error after recovery from the recoil of a shot.

f. Recheck after each error is found until no error exists.

3. The shooter must always remember that the improvement of his marksmanship skill requires an unceasing search for an even better stance and position. The position and stance assumed must not be considered as something constant. As marksmanship skill develops, changes in the stance and position are necessary in order to improve performance.

4. Many expert marksmen, as a result of long and persistent training have completely developed their stance and position to the point of automation, sometimes not even noting its individual shortcomings. It sometimes happens that some experts, even though they know about their shortcomings, do not attach the proper importance to them. Only when the individual shortcomings in position or stance become a serious hindrance to their progress do they begin to change. The overwhelming majority of the leading shooters actually work seriously and creatively to improve themselves by evaluation of their position and stance.

5. Young shooters must not blindly copy, and instructors and coaches must not mechanically, without any analysis, instill in their pupils a particular variation of position or stance. It is necessary to make an intelligent approach to the problem of selecting the particular stance and position that is acceptable to oneself, taking from the experts desirable aspects and rejecting undesirable ones.

C. GRIP.

The proper grip is one which provides the shooter with the maximum control of the weapon. To maintain a natural sight alignment, he must hold the weapon firmly and be able to apply positive, straight to the rear pressure on the trigger that will not disturb sight alignment.

1. Uniformity: For maximum control, all of the requirements for a proper grip must be uniformly applied at all times.

2. Requirements: The proper grip on a pistol is one that meets the following requirements:

a. The grip should be such that the front and rear sights will stay in natural alignment without any extra effort to maintain the relationship. Without this feature, there will be a tendency for the front sight to move over to one side of the rear sight notch, or be moved above or below the horizontal surface of the rear sight. Sight alignment, quickly regained after recoil without the need for correction, speeds up recovery and improves timed and rapid fire control. Maintaining sight alignment should be an effortless action before the next shot. Positive trigger pressure can be applied if the sight alignment is being maintained without effort. Sight alignment is easier to maintain if no adjustments are necessary such as moving the wrist or head.

b. Grip the pistol firmly enough while firing a shot so that shifting or slipping of the grip will not cause loss of control of the pistol. Recovery from recoil for the next shot in sustained fire is seriously hampered by the loss of sight alignment. The trigger pressure under these conditions is usually reluctant and timid. Unless the proper grip can be renewed quickly, (next to impossible in the middle of a timed or rapid fire string) maintaining sight alignment during the application of positive trigger pressure is a difficult operation. The tighter the grip, short of setting up a tremble, the better the control. The degree of pressure that should be exerted in gripping the pistol is determined by the condition of the muscles that do the gripping. Frequent practice, experience and certain exercises promote a strong grip and have a bearing on when a tremble will begin.

c. There must be no change in the tightness of the grip because a variation of gripping pressure will adversely effect sight alignment. Any degree of tightening or loosening of the grip from an established grasp will cause the sights to move out of alignment. The pressure of the grip must remain constant. It cannot be increased or decreased as trigger pressure is being applied because sight alignment will be altered.

d. The trigger finger should apply positive pressure on the trigger as an independent action, completely free of the other muscles of the shooting hand. The trigger finger should not touch the stock or the frame of the pistol because of the added friction and drag on applying trigger pressure. Dry fire a few shots watching the front sight carefully. If the front sight moves at the instant the hammer falls, reposition the trigger finger to the left or right, up or down, on the face of the trigger. Repeat the dry firing and adjusting the position of trigger finger until the release of the hammer causes no movement of the front sight in the rear sight notch.

e. There can be no variation in the grip from one shot to the next, from one series of shots to the next, from one day's shooting to the next, ad infinitum. In the final analysis, there is only one correct grip for each shooter. Each type of pistol, caliber .22, caliber .38, caliber .45 has its peculiarities and the shooter must adapt to each. The proper grip can be discovered through trial and error, practice and analysis. It must become, by extensive use, a familiar operation that eventually can be assumed without much difficulty. When the experienced shooter checks his grip out before shooting, it seldom needs adjustment. One of the frequent variations of grip that plagues new shooters is the grasping of the pistol grip with the hand slightly displaced to the right or left from the normal. As a result the placement of the trigger finger on the trigger will be different, thereby jeopardizing the requirement that the trigger be pressed straight to the rear.

f. The grip must be as comfortable as possible. The muscles of the hand and lower arm, after sufficient time has passed for the hand to become accustomed to the added stress, should experience little discomfort from the way the pistol is placed in the hand. If the grip is awkward and possible cramping and the hand muscles continue to tire easily, look for another solution or use an exercise device to strengthen the hand. To avoid the formation of painful, blisters, callouses and cracked tissue, reduce the tendency of the skin to stretch. Tautly stretched skin may also pull or exert force on the pistol frame in such a way as to cause sight alignment deviation. An equalization of the stretching of the skin and muscles of the gripping hand is paramount. Straight-in contact should exist between the skin of the fingers and palm and the surfaces of the frame and grips when the gripping pressures are brought to bear; not a sideward, sliding or grazing pressure.

g. The force of recoil must be controlled by being transmitted straight to the rear into the shooting arm. Recoil against the base of the thumb, which causes the weapon to twist in the hand, will allow a shift or grip and/or a bending of the wrist. Either event jeopardizes quick recovery from recoil in timed and rapid fire. The pistol should be held by being gripped normally, not by a choking grasp that endeavors to press on the stock in an all enveloping grab. The best points of pressure to hold the sight in alignment are the semi-flat grips on each side of the frame. However, the gripping hand cannot exert equal pressure on each of these surfaces simultaneously and such pressure would not overcome the effect of recoil. Therefore, the obvious pressure points of the shooting hand that will channel the effect of recoil straight to the rear and allow relative ease in maintaining sight alignment are: the middle bones of the three lower fingers, the base of the thumb high on the stock, the depression on the center of the heel of the hand, and last, the base joints of the four fingers along the upper palm. The primary pressure points on the .45 caliber pistol are the front surface of the grip and the mainspring housing-grip safety surfaces. The secondary points are: high on the left side of the stock near the slide lock and the forward curve of the right grip, each of which have to have gripping pressure applied equally to prevent loosening of the over all grip, and to maintain sight alignment.

h. Holding the grip too long without an occasional relaxation will result in early fatigue. Fatigue destroys control. Excessive force of gripping for control of the pistol assures that fatigue will exist if the gripping power of the hand is weak. Undue fatigue in the muscles of the hand and forearm will also cause erratic application of trigger pressure. The tremble level is lowered to a point where the shooter cannot hold the pistol still, even for a few seconds, while trigger pressure is being applied.

3. Method of getting the proper grip: The proper grip must conform to all of the foregoing requirements plus it must be a hard grip and it must be adapted to the hand of the individual shooter.

NOTE: FOR THIS INSTRUCTION IN OBTAINING THE PROPER GRIP, THE WEAPON IS THE .45 CALIBER SERVICE PISTOL. THE FOLLOWING STEP-BY-STEP SEQUENCE WILL PROVIDE THE PROPER GRIP:

a. With the non-shooting hand, pick up the pistol by the barrel end of the slide, being careful not to mar the blackened sight and keep the muzzle pointed down range.

11

b. Spread the index finger and thumb of the shooting hand apart to form a "V," with the thumb held slightly lower than the index finger.

c. Bend the wrist slightly downward to obtain proper angle of contact.

d. Fit the pistol into the "V" of the thumb and index fingers by seating the grip safety straight and firmly into the loose "web" of skin in the "V."

e. Press downward on the barrel to pivot and push the mainspring housing firmly against the inside of the bulge of flesh at the base of the thumb and into the depression in the approximate center of the heel of the palm.

f. Stretch the fingers forward, letting the trigger finger come to rest flat against the pistol frame just above the trigger guard. Safety dictates the trigger not be contacted at this time.

g. The lower three fingers should come to rest closely touching each other, with the center bone of each finger resting on the curved front surface or "front strap" of the receiver. Little or no pressure should be exerted on the finger tips extending around the front strap to the surface of the left handgrip. Pressure exerted on the front strap by the little finger should be lighter than that brought to bear by the middle and ring fingers. Too much pressure with the little finger may cause the muzzle to depress slightly, resulting in the front sight aligning low in the rear sight notch.

h. The thumb should be raised to a level higher than the index or trigger finger. Only the joint at the middle of the thumb is high against the stock in the vicinity of the slide safety. The end of the thumb is turned up and away from the stock as it has no function. Pressure exerted on the side of the pistol by the end of the thumb has a tendency to disturb sight alignment. The thumb should not exert great pressure on the side of the pistol as early fatigue will result. Only required substantial supporting force should be exerted to hold the weapon firmly in place in the shooting hand.

i. A controlling grip can be affected by the three lower fingers directing primary pressure on the front strap straight to the rear, pressing the mainspring housing and grip safety firmly against the side of the center depression and the heel of the palm at the base of the thumb, and the loose flesh in the "V" of the thumb and index finger, respectively. This can be compared to a vise with the inner surfaces of the palm as the stationary jaw of the vise and the three lower fingers pressing on the front strap of the pistol as the moving jaw.

j. The non-shooting hand should be used to adjust the "fit" of the pistol into the shooting hand. A slight rotation of the weapon in the gripping hand as it is alternately gripping and releasing will allow the equalizing of a forceful grasp. The gripping hand must reach around to the right far enough to allow the trigger finger to reach into the trigger guard and also to position itself on the trigger at the exact point at which the trigger pressure can be applied straight to the rear. According to the size of the hand, the trigger finger will apply pressure with the tip, ball of the first section or the crook of the first joint or elsewhere. The primary concern is not what portion or spot along the trigger finger is the standard point of contact, but at what spot on the finger you can bisect the trigger, press straight to the rear without disturbing sight alignment.

k. When the "fit" is correct, remove the trigger finger from the trigger, free the pistol from the non-shooting hand and tighten the grip with great force until a tremor is noticed. Release a small percentage of this gripping pressure immediately, enough so that the tremor disappears and leaves the shooter with a hard, solid grasp that will result in absolute control. The tighter the grip, the better the control. The shooter is now exerting correct pressure for maximum recoil control.

4. Checking For Proper Grip: The proper grip is a natural grip that will meet all the requirements in paragraph 2, above. To assure a proper grip, it should be checked against the requirements. A deciding factor in knowing whether your grip is proper is one of familiarity. By use of the proper grip innumerable times, a flaw is immediately sensed.

a. To assure the sights will stay in alignment, the following test is made: extend the shooting arm and observe the sight alignment. If the front and rear sights are out of alignment, grasp the barrel with the non-shooting hand, loosen the grip sufficiently to slide the pistol in the hand, rotating it slightly away from the direction of error in sight alignment. Regrasp the pistol firmly and extend the arm. Check the alignment without an effort being made to align them by wrist or head movement. If the alignment is natural, you may check for maintenance of sight alignment. With the arm extended, close the eyes, raise and lower the arm and settle. Open the eyes and observe. If the alignment has deviated, reposition the pistol in the shooting hand and repeat the closed eye test until natural alignment of the front and rear sights is achieved and maintained. During shooting, a constant check should be conducted of the tendency of the sights to continue to align themselves. The grip obtained at the beginning of shooting will not necessarily remain correct because the jolting recoil and build-up of fatigue will require correction to the grip to maintain sight alignment.

b. To check for a grip firm enough to prevent shifting after making sure the pistol is unloaded, have the coach bump the pistol rather forcefully, up or to the side with the heel of his hand. Also, have the coach grasp the pistol by the barrel and make an effort to tear it from your grasp.

c. To check for variations in tightness or correctness of grip, it is best to dry fire a few shots before live shooting starts and watch for slight viarations in sight alignment.

d. Checking for independent trigger action should be accomplished before shooting by a visual check of the trigger finger clearance from the grip. Check by dry firing to detect any drag or undue friction noticed in the trigger. Also, check for a sympathetic tightening of the muscles of the hand as trigger pressure is applied. This can cause as much disturbance of sight alignment as the failure to press the trigger straight to the rear.

e. The rapid onset of fatigue and soreness of the shooting hand is usually the result of an incorrect grip.

f. Checking for straight to the rear recoil directly into the shooting arm and shoulder can best be done in practice with an unloaded pistol by having a coach or team mate stand in front of you and forcefully and abruptly push against the muzzle of your tightly gripped pistol driving it straight back toward your shoulder in simulation of recoil action.

5. Aids to Developing a Good Grip: The great pistol shooters have: strong hands and a hard grip; a method of gripping without change unless analysis dictates a change that will improve it; a different grip mastered for each shape of stock or different type of pistol; molded, shaped or custom grips, that fit perfectly; and if they use powdered rosin or a like substance, they use it everytime the hand becomes moist before they grip the pistol.

a. The "top guns" have a grip like a vise. Exercise devices such as rubber balls, spring grip builders, etc. will develop a strong grip. Exercise devices require constant use. Another approach, to reduce reliance on artificial exercisers, is to engage in work or a sport that places demands on your manual strength and dexterity, for example, chopping wood, digging in the garden, using hand clippers on the hedge; playing tennis, baseball, pingpong, etc. Use of the hands in meticulous work also develops an exacting touch and coordination that is valuable to the pistol shooter.

b. Never thoughtlessly change your grip. A correct grip is a precious commodity. It evolves from much hard work, thinking, and planning, plus painstaking analysis. Each satisfactory grip found among the better shooters comes from trial and error. The good grip that is the end product of much effort should not be changed except when sharply critical analysis dictates a change that will improve it. The shooter who is desperately changing his grip hoping that he will chance upon the right solution will generally lower his scores. In the event that a better score is fired under these conditions it comes on an occasional basis with no tangible reason for the improvement. Analysis and trial, in a never ending quest to improve your marksmanship, is the answer.

c. A modification of the shooter's proper grip is necessary on different types of pistols. The firmness of the grip remains the same for all calibers and types of pistols and revolvers, but nature of the grasp must correspond to the shape and size of the grips in meeting all the requirements of the proper grip. For example, the caliber .22 grip is sometimes found to be smaller in circumference than a caliber .45 pistol. In this instance, the reach of the lower three fingers may extend further around the stock, resulting in one of the primary pressure points (the middle bones of each of the three lower fingers) coming to rest beyond and partially around to the left side of the front strap. Pressure exerted thusly would not be straight to the rear. As it is fully applied in the normal grip, it would no doubt effect the natural alignment of the sights. Also, shooters with small hands have trouble with stocks of varying sizes. One example is having to compromise, due to a short trigger finger which can reach the trigger only with the finger tip, between a straight to the rear trigger pressure and the best position of the pistol in the shooting hand that tends to give natural sight alignment.

d. Shaped, molded or tailored custom grips are required to fit perfectly. Fitted grips are primarily used to help the shooter who can't consistently duplicate the proper grip when using standard factory grips. The individual shooter must first decide what features and characteristics of a shaped grip suit his hand. Stocks can be made to fit exactly, but it is a difficult job. Only an experienced shooter is capable of knowing what he actually needs in a custom grip, because only he knows what his proper grip looks and feels like.

e. Powdered rosin dusted on the hand can help to maintain a solid, controlling grip but it is not absolutely necessary. Normally, a strong hand and the checkering and stippling on the stocks and metal surfaces is sufficient. In hot weather when the hand may perspire or a hand that becomes wet in the rain may cause slippage, powdered rosin or a like substance, that will temporarily dry the skin of the palm and fingers, is then justified.

In the final analysis, there is only one correct grip for you. It is one that is firm; affords the individual shooter the maximum degree of control over maintaining sight alignment and allows positive, straight to the rear pressure on the trigger without disturbing sight alignment.

D. BREATH CONTROL.

The correct method of breathing is an essential part of the shooter's system of control. Most pistol shooters know less about the proper method of breath control than of any of the other fundamentals

The object of proper breath control is to enable the pistol shooter to hold his breath with a comfortable feeling long enough to fire one shot slow fire; five shots in twenty seconds timed fire; or five shots in ten seconds rapid fire without loss of the ability to hold still or concentrate on sight alignment.

1. To be Effective, Breath Control Must Be Employed Systematically and Uniformly: The ability to concentrate and maintain rhythm is aided.

a. Promote a steady hold. It is generally known that one must not breathe during aiming. Breathing is accompanied by the rhythmical movement of the chest, abdomen, and the shoulders. This causes the pistol to move about excessively, making it almost impossible to produce an accurate shot. Therefore, one must not simultaneously breathe and try to fire a shot, but must endeavor to hold the breath for a short period of time.

b. The physiological processes involved in breathing: The shooter however, must not view the breathing process solely from the movement of the chest and the gun. He must not forget that the process of breathing, which consists of a combination of processes which occur constantly in the human body, determine in general the condition of the human being. Therefore, proper breathing is of great importance during shooting exercises which last several hours. Incorrect breathing technique has an adverse effect upon shooting, especially if the concentration is disturbed by sensing of the need to breathe.

(1) During the process of breathing, there is an alternating increase and decrease in the volume of the chest, as a result the person inhales and exhales. A person inhales when the dimensions of the chest increase. Once inside the lungs, the air provides oxygen to the blood and in turn it absorbs carbon dioxide and aqueous vapors. Exhalation occurs when all the muscles relax, the diaphragm presses upward, and, under the action of the weight of the chest and the elasticity of the lungs, air is forced out of the body. Exhaling does not require muscular effort; it occurs as the result of the resiliency of the ribs and the muscular tissues and the elasticity of the lungs.

(2) When breathing calmly a person produces an average of 12 - 13 respiratory cycles a minute. Consequently, one respiratory cycle lasts 4 - 5 seconds. If one traces the respiratory cycle, it is not difficult to note that the strained position of inhalation is replaced very quickly by exhalation. The very next inhalation begins after a respiratory pause of 2 to 3 seconds, (figure 1-7) during which time the carbon dioxide accumulates in the lungs. The duration of the respiratory pause is determined by the ratio of oxygen and carbon dioxide in the air remaining in the lungs.

14

Figure 1-7. Scheme of a Person's Breathing.

(3) The respiratory pause and the problems of the ventilation of the lungs are of great importance to the shooter. It is obvious that during aiming and applying pressure on the trigger, the breath must be held only after the shooter has exhaled, timing it so that the breath is held at the moment of the natural respiratory pause. During that time the muscles are not strained and are in a relaxed state.

c. A person can prolong by several seconds this respiratory pause, that is, hold his breath comfortably for 15 - 20 seconds, without any special labor and without experiencing unpleasant sensations. This time is more than adequate to produce a shot or shots. Experienced shooters usually take a deep breath before firing and then, exhaling slowly, hold their breath gradually, relax and concentrate their entire attention upon sight alignment and the smooth application of pressure on the trigger (Figure 1-8).

Figure 1-8. Scheme of the Manner in Which A Person Holds His Breath in Order to Produce a Shot.

2. Recommended method:

a. Prior to fire commands:

(1) When expelling the air from the lungs before aimining, no effort whatever must be exerted. The exhaling must be natural and free, as in ordinary breathing. The air must not be held in the lungs; incomplete exhaling before aiming leads to straining and to stimulation of the nerve centers regulating the breathing, and the shooter's concentration on aiming is distracted.

(2) In order to make sure that during prolonged firing the interruption of the rhythm of breathing does not have an influence upon the shooter, the breath must not be held for an excessive period when trying to fire a slow fire shot. If the shooter does not produce a shot in 8 - 10 seconds, he must stop aiming and take another breath.

(3) Before holding his breath for the next shot he must empty his lungs well, taking several deep breaths. The same should be done between shots and strings of shots throughout the firing. This facilitates the lengthening of the respiratory pause before aiming and provides for regular rest between shots and strings. The oxygen level in the blood is slightly increased. As a result the shooter is relaxed and comfortable during all shooting without excessive and premature fatigue.

15

b. During the fire commands: Take a deeper than normal breath at the command, "READY ON THE RIGHT, " take another at "READY ON THE LEFT, " extend your pistol and take the final breath and exhale to the point of comfort at "READY ON THE FIRING LINE. "

As the shooter gains experience in proper breath control, he will find that he will hold his breath, or extend his normal respiratory pause, without being too conscious of the action and allow intense concentration on sight alignment and trigger pressure.

c. During actual firing: The shooter should not be conscious of the need to breathe. If during practice a shooter finds that he cannot hold his breath the twenty seconds necessary to fire a timed fire string, he should make a practice of firing his timed fire strings in less than twenty seconds However, if during a timed or rapid fire string, the shooter feels compelled to breathe, he should take a short breath quickly and continue to fire. This causes a lapse of concentration on sight alignment and should not be the normal technique used.

CHAPTER II

SIGHT ALIGNMENT

Sight alignment is the most important contribution to firing an accurate shot.

In order for the bullet to hit the center of the target, the shooter must aim the pistol and give the barrel a definite direction relative to the target.

In theory, accurate aiming is achieved when the shooter places in exact alignment, the rear sight with the top and ideas of the front sight, and holds them in alignment in the aiming area.

A requisite for correct aiming is the ability to maintain the relationship between the front and rear sights.

When aiming, the front sight is positioned in the middle of the rear sight notch with an equal light space on each side. The horizontal top surface of the front sight is on the same level as the top horizontal surface of the rear sight notch (figure 2-1.)

A. RELATIONSHIP OF SIGHTS. It is necessary to be acutely aware of the relationship of the rear sight to the clearly defined front sight. Normal vision is such that the rear sight of the pistol will be as nearly in focus as the front sight. Some shooters may be able to see only the notch of the rear sight in sharp focus; the outer extremities may become slightly blurred.

Front sight   Rear sight   Combined   Target   Combined in center of aim- ing area   With minimum arc of movement (exaggerated)

Figure 2-1. The Relationship of the Sights.

1. Angular Shift Error: If the shooter does not observe correct aiming (maintaining the top surface of the centered front sight on a level with the top of the rear sight and equal light space on each side of the front sight), there will be few accurate shots. Most often, he locates the front sight in a different position in the rear notch. This accounts for a greater dispersion of shots on the target, since the bullets will deviate in the direction in which the front sight is positioned in the notch. (Figure 2-2). This aiming error is known as angular shift error.

Figure 2-2. Displacement of the Bullet When There is Angular Shift Error in the Alignment of the Front Sight.

2. Parallel Shift Error: If the hold (arc of movement) is deviating in near parallel error from the center of the aiming area, the shooter should know that these deflections will not lower the score to the extent of angular shift error. Therefore, sight alignment is the most critical of the two. Thus, the accuracy of a shot depends mainly upon the shooter's ability to consistently maintain correct sight alignment. The main effort should be toward keeping your sights aligned. Holding the pistol *perfectly still is desirable but it is not mandatory.*

Good sight alignment.
Zeroed for 6 o'clock
area hold. Shot breaks
high in a hold error.

High front sight error.
Zeroed for 6 o'clock area
hold. Hold is good.

Figure 2-3. Displacement of the Bullet When The Pistol is Shifted: (a) Parallel, (b) Angular:

B. POINT OF FOCUS.

Correct sight alignment must be thoroughly understood and practiced. It appears on the surface as a simple thing - this lining up of two objects, front and rear sights. The problem lies in the difficulty in maintaining these two sights in precise alignment while the shooter is maintaining a minimum arc of movement and pressing the trigger to cause the hammer to fall without disturbing sight alignment.

The solution is partly in focusing the eye on the front sight during the delivery of the shot.

Figure 2-4a. Impossible! The Human Eye Cannot Focus On A Close-UP Object and A Distant Object Simultaneously.

Figure 2-4b. Improper. Control of sight alignment is not precise. Distinct focus on target renders sight indistinct. Error incorporated here is the same as Figs 34a and is not as readily apparent.

Figure 2-4c. Proper. Control alignment is precise. Focus limited to front sight only, renders the sights distinct and target indistinct and sight relationship can be controlled constantly.

1. It is imperative to maintain "front sight point of focus" throughout the sighting and aiming of the pistol. The shooter must concentrate on maintaining the correct relationship between front and rear sight, and the point of focus must be on the front sight during the short period required to deliver the shot. If the focus is displaced forward, and the target is momentarily in clear focus, the ability of the shooter to achieve correct sight alignment is jeopardized for that moment. Frequently, this is the moment that the pistol fires. A controlled, accurate shot is impossible under these conditions.

2. When the eye is focused on the target the relatively small movement of the arm appears magnified. However, when the eye is correctly focused on the front sight this movement appears to have been reduced.

C. CONCENTRATION.

1. If the sights are incorrectly aligned, the net result is an inaccurate shot. Carelessness in obtaining correct sight alignment can usually be traced to the shooter's failure to realize its importance. Many shooters will, in the initial phase of holding, line up the sights in a perfect manner. However, as the firing progresses, and the shooter is concentrating on delivering the shot, he often loses correct sight alignment which he attained in the initial phase of his hold. Usually, when the shooter is unable to maintain a pin-point hold, his concentration on sight alignment wavers. An accurate shot is lost because the shooter is thinking of his arc of movement and not the perfection of sight alignment.

2. Another factor which contributes to the deterioration of sight alignment, is the feeling of anxiety which arises over the apparently stationary pressure on the trigger when attempting to fire. An impulse is generated to get more pressure on the trigger, so that the shot will be delivered. When the shooter thinks about increasing the trigger pressure, a degree of the intense concentration required to maintain correct sight alignment is lost. Even if trigger control and the hold are good, the net result will be a poor shot. Sight alignment must remain uppermost in the shooter's mind throughout the

19

firing of the shot. Positive trigger pressure must be applied involuntarily. Consistently accurate shots are produced when the shooter maintains intense concentration on sight alignment during the application of trigger pressure, while experiencing a minimum arc of movement. Control of the shot is lessened in direct proportion to the loss of concentration on sight alignment.

    3. <u>The average, advanced shooter is probably limited in sustained concentration to a period of 3 to 6 seconds.</u>   This short space of time is the optimum period in which a controlled shot can be delivered. This concentration interval should be attained simultaneously with acquiring a minimum arc of movement, a point of focus, satisfactory sight alignment, and the involuntary starting of positive trigger pressure. If exact sight alignment is maintained, and the trigger pressure remains positive, the shot will break during the limited time the shooter is able to control his uninterrupted concentration. Result! A dead center hit on the target.

    D. THE EYE.

    The principal difficulties which confront the shooter during aiming are determined to a great extent by the inherent characteristics of the eye and its work as an optical apparatus. All shooters should familiarize themselves with the optical properties of the human eye as explained in Annex II, entitled "Optical Properties of the Human Eye Relevant to Sight Alignment."

CHAPTER III

TRIGGER CONTROL

A. GENERAL.

Correct trigger control must be employed in conjunction with all other fundamentals of shooting. The physical act of applying pressure on the trigger to deliver an accurate shot may vary from individual to individual. Proper trigger control for each individual gradually assumes uniformity when the techniques of proper application are mastered. Many shooters, for example, maintain a degree of trigger control with a relatively light grip, while another shooter may use a very tight grip. Some shooters prefer to apply consistent trigger pressure at a rapid rate, while maintaining correct sight alignment. For another shooter, a slower, deliberate application may achieve the same results. An ever increasing number of shooters use the positive approach to trigger control, that is, once it is initiated, it becomes an uninterrupted, constantly increasing pressure until the weapon fires.

Trigger control is of very great importance in producing an accurate shot. When the shooter exerts pressure on the trigger, he must do so in a manner that does not alter the sight alignment, or position of the pistol. Consequently, the shooter must be able to exert smooth, even pressure to the trigger. Furthermore, the trigger must be pressed in conjunction with maximum concentration, peak visual perception of sight alignment and minimum arc of movement.

In order to produce an accurate shot, the shooter must carry out many diverse, but related, actions. Fulfilling this action is compounded by the fact that the pistol is in some degree of motion throughout the period of sighting and aiming. The movement varies according to the stability of the shooter's stance. Consequently, the sight alignment deviates from the aiming area. Often it will move through the aiming area, pausing only for a short period of time in perfect alignment with the target. It is impossible to determine when, and for how long the properly aligned sights will stay in the center of the aiming area. This difficulty is aggravated further by the fact that the shooter is trying to execute coordinated actions when reflex action seeks to contradict them. Such a situation requires the development of conditioned reflexes, and improvement of coordination.

The coordinated action of correct aiming, timely pressure on the trigger, and the correct delivery of the shot is difficult and can be accomplished only by overcoming former uncoordinated reflexes or by acquiring new ones. Only through constant training and attention to accepted techniques can these new reflexes be acquired. The peculiar nature and characteristics of the human nervous system are covered in detail in Annex III entitled, "Processes of the Human Nervous System Relevant to Equilibrium, Trigger Control and Hearing."

B. FACTORS PROVIDING FOR THE CORRECT CONTROL OF THE TRIGGER.

The pressure put on the trigger must come from independent movement of the trigger finger only. The gripping fingers and the thumb do not move or tighten. Keep the grip pressure constant. Align the sight, settle into your normal aiming area and exert positive, uninterrupted, increasing pressure, straight to the rear, until the hammer falls. You must not look for a perfect sight picture combination of rear sight-front sight-bull's eye. Instead, focus your eye on the front sight, keeping it perfectly aligned in the rear sight notch. The blur of the out-of-focus target may move about slightly, but this movement is relatively unimportant. Any time the weapon is fired with good sight alignment within the normal arc of movement and it is a surprise shot, the shot will be a good one, and will hit the target within your ability to hold.

Trigger control has a series of actions that take place if a smooth release of the firing mechanism is accomplished.

1. Slack and Initial Pressure: Any free movement of the trigger, known as slack, has to be taken up prior to a light initial pressure. This action assures that the tolerances in the firing mechanism linkage are taken up and are in firm contact before positive trigger pressure is applied.

Initial pressure is an automatic, lightly applied pressure, approximately one-fourth or less of the total required to fire the weapon. This careful action is an aid in the positive pressure that will release the hammer quickly and smoothly.

21

In order to fire a controlled shot the shooter must learn to increase the pressure on the trigger positively, smoothly, gradually, and evenly. This does not mean, however, that the trigger must be pressed slowly. It must be pressed smoothly, without interruption, but the release of the trigger must take no more than 2 to 5 seconds. Numerous accurate rapid fire strings of five shots in ten seconds are fired in a cycle that allows only one second or less to employ the principals of correct trigger control.

Smooth trigger action makes special demands on the trigger finger when pressing upon the trigger; its correct functioning determines to a great extent the quality of the shot. The most carefully attained sight alignment will be spoiled by the slightest error in the movement of the trigger finger.

2. ·Function of Proper Grip: In order for the index finger to be able to perform its function without spoiling the aim, it is first necessary to have the hand grasp the pistol correctly and create the proper support; permitting the trigger finger to overcome the trigger tension. The pistol grips must be grasped tightly but without any tremor. It is also necessary that the index finger clears the side of the stock. The movement of the index finger must be independent as it presses on the trigger, and also not cause any lateral change to the sight alignment.

3. Proper Placement of the Trigger Finger: It is necessary to apply pressure on the trigger with either the first bone section of the index finger, or with the first joint. The trigger must be pressed straight to the rear. If the finger presses the trigger to the side, undesirable things will happen. The weight of trigger pull will increase; because of additional friction on certain parts of the trigger mechanism an otherwise flawless trigger action will take on the characteristics of a poor trigger when side pressure is exerted on the trigger. Another consideration is the effect that side pressure has on sight alignment. Only slight pressure to the side is required to bring about an error in sight alignment. The prime cause of exerting pressure to the side is improper placement of the trigger finger.

Figure 3-1. Correct Placement of the Index Finger on the Trigger.
(a) With Joint of Index Finger.   (b) With First Bone Section of Index Finger.

Ideal trigger finger placement may be modified to a degree by the requirement that the grip provide a natural alignment of the front and rear sights. The shooter frequently must make a compromise to overcome the undesirable effects of not being able to utilize each factor to full advantage.

4. Coordination: It must be emphasized that match shooting is successful only when all the control factors are consistently in coordination.

Ability to control the trigger smoothly is not sufficient in itself to produce an accurate shot. The trigger must be activated in conjunction with correct sight alignment, minimum arc of movement, and maximum undisturbed concentration. This might be called cadence, rhythm or timing. Under any name, it comes only to those who practice frequently. Occasional ability is not the answer to championship shooting. A three-gun aggregate requires 270 successful results. Consistent, exacting performance is enhanced by an ability to compensate automatically for errors. It is necessary during firing to press the trigger under varying conditions of pistol movement in conjunction with correct sight alignment. In order to apply coordinated pressure on the trigger, the shooter must wait for definite times when all factors and conditions are favorable. Frequently, it will be impossible to exercise maximum control. However, the shooter must never attempt to fire until he has completely settled into a minimum arc of movement.

C. APPLICATION OF TRIGGER PRESSURE.

1. Positive Uninterrupted Trigger Pressure-Surprise shot method-is primarily the act of completing the firing of the shot once starting the application of trigger pressure. The shooter is committed to an unchanging rate of pressure, no speed up, no slowdown or stopping. The trigger pressure is of an uninterrupted nature because it is not applied initially unless conditions are settled and near perfect. If the perfect conditions deteriorate, the shooter should not fire, but bench the weapon, relax, replan, and start again.

In instances when the pistol is stable and steady, and the periods of minimum arc of movement are of longer duration, it is immaterial whether the release of the trigger is completed a second sooner or a second later. Anytime that the shot is fired with minimum arc of movement and the sights are in alignment, it will be a good shot. Therefore, when the shooter has established stable minimum arc of movement and sight alignment, he must immediately begin to press on the trigger, smoothly but positively, and straight to the rear without stopping, until a shot is produced. This method of controlling the trigger action will give the shooter a surprise break of the shot before any muscular reflex can disturb sight alignment.

Figure 3-2. Surprise Shot with Positive Uninterrupted Trigger Pressure.

2. Interrupted Application of Trigger Pressure or the "Point" shooting Method: This is a method of trigger control not recommended, although used by some shooters. Some shooters think they can pick the trigger release time even after years of experience.

a. The shooter will align the sights and exert initial pressure on the trigger. He will then make every effort to hold the weapon motionless. During extremely brief moments of motionlessness, pressure is applied on the trigger. If the sight alignment changes and is not perfect, or the arc of movement of the weapon increases, the pressure on the trigger is halted and trigger tension maintained. When sight alignment is again perfect and movement diminishes, pressure on the trigger is resumed until the shot breaks, or after the slack in the trigger is taken up, initial pressure is applied and the shot released by a single swift movement of the trigger finger when there is a decrease in the minimum arc of movement. In this case the presence of perfect sight alignment is not considered essential in initiating trigger action. Abrupt action in applying trigger pressure will disturb the existing sight alignment and other fundamental control factors are subordinated to a minimum arc of movement. The application of all other fundamentals is required regardless of whether or not they are optimum.

Figure 3-3. Application of Trigger Pressure When Based on Perfect Sight Picture.

23

b. While applying positive trigger pressure straight to the rear, if any thought enters the shooter's mind to speed up or slow down this trigger pressure, it will result in the concentration on sight alignment being broken down.

c. The decision to increase the trigger pressure may result in a reflex action commonly known as anticipation and usually results in heeling the shot (The bullet strikes the target at approximately one o'clock). The recoil becomes more imminent and the brain will send a signal for the arm and hand muscles to react prematurely a split second before the shot is fired; resulting in frequent bad shots and low scores.

Figure 3-4. Shot Fired With Interrupted Trigger Pressure Compared to Shot Fired
With Uninterrupted Positive Trigger Control.

D. ERRORS MADE IN TRIGGER CONTROL AND MEANS OF COMBATTING THEM.

1. The most serious and disrupting error made by the shooter is jerking - that is, the abrupt application of pressure on the trigger accompanied with muscular action of the hand and arm muscles.

If jerking was limited to abrupt pressure on the trigger, and the rapid displacement of the axis of the bore, it would cause only part of the results.

a. Jerking is usually accompanied by:

(1) The sharp straining of all the muscles in the arm and shoulder.

(2) The abrupt tightening of the hand on the grip.

(3) Failure to press the trigger directly to the rear.

All of these factors, taken together, lead to a great shifting of the pistol to the side and down and only a very poor shot can result.

b. Most frequently, jerking is observed in new shooters. Usually, because of a large arc of movement, favorable moments for producing a good shot are of very short duration.

c. The cause of trigger-jerking, is the practice of "snatching a ten-pointer," as the expression goes. The shooter tries to fire at the moment when the centered front sight, as it moves back and forth, passes under the lower edge of the bull's eye, or comes to a stop, for a brief time, near the center of the aiming area. Since these moments are fleeting the inexperienced shooter strives to exert all the necessary pressure on the trigger at that time. This rapid and abrupt trigger pressure is accompanied not only by the work of the muscles in the index finger, but also by the sympathetic action of a number of other muscles. The involuntary action of these muscles produces the "jerk," and the inaccurate shot that results. The young shooter, in anticipation of the recoil of the pistol and its loud noise, strains his muscles by flinching, to counteract the anticipated recoil. This is also known as heeling the shot.

d. Practice has shown that a young shooter must be warned sufficiently early in his training about the dangers of jerking the trigger and effective steps taken to instruct him in the correct technique of accurate shooting.

e. Difficulty in detecting errors in trigger control is frequently because the pistol shifted during recoil and errors are not recognized. The shooter has a more difficult time in evaluating his actions than a coach, and often does not realize that he is jerking the trigger, blinking his eyes, or straining his arm and shoulder muscles.

f. The easiest way to correct jerking in the young shooter is by the coaching of an experienced coach. A coach can more readily detect errors and correct habits that will produce poo. trigger control. Frequently a shooter does not consider it necessary to prove conclusively whether o. not they are jerking on the trigger. It is necessary, though, to know that if he does not get rid of the detrimental habit of jerking on the trigger, he will never succeed in achieving good results.

g. Signs of jerking are an increase in the size of the area of the shot group or shots off to the side which are not called there; chiefly to the left and down (for right handers). To correct this condition, the shooter must make a change in his training exercises, but in no instance must he stop them.

(1) Dry-fire practice will enable the nervous system to rest from the recoil of the shot. By this practice some of the reflexes which are detrimental to firing (tensing of the arm in order to counteract the recoil, the straining of the muscles in expectation of the shot, blinking from the noise of the shot), are not being developed. They will, in fact, begin to decrease and may completely disappear.

(2) Secondly, the shooter may continue regular training, but occasionally he may practice "dry". This way, he will not lose the stability of this position, as well as the useful reflexes which the shooter has developed during the process of previous firings.

(3) By aiming carefully and noting attentively everything that happens to the pistol when he presses on the trigger, the shooter will discover his errors and eliminate them. Training by means of ball and dummy and dry firing is of great benefit. It makes it possible to develop correctly and carefully the technique of pressing the trigger, and contributes to acquiring proper habits in controlling the trigger.

(4) When beginning to use dry firing the shooter must first overcome the desire to "grab" for a shot when the centered front sight is under the bull's eye. Despite the arc of movement the shooter must teach himself only to press smoothly on the trigger and to use the uninterrupted positive control method of trigger action. When the smooth control of the trigger again becomes habitual and he no longer has to devote special attention to it, he can again shoot live cartridges. After starting again to shoot live cartridges, the first training exercises should involve firing at a square of blank white paper, rather than at a target with a black aiming area. Simultaneously, the shooter must devote special attention to analyzing his performance, counteract the desire to jerk on the trigger, and be conscious of reacting incorrectly to the firing of a shot.

2. Another error committed by a shooter when controlling the trigger is "holding too long," that is, the drawn out action of pressing the trigger.

a. A consequence of holding too long is that the shooter does not have enough air to hold his breath, his eye becomes fatigued, and his visual acuity decreases. In addition, his stance loses part of its stability. Consequently, when he holds too long, the shooter presses on the trigger under unfavorable conditions.

b. Holding too long is a consequence of excessively slow and cautious pressure on the trigger. This is caused by the shooter's fear of producing a bad shot. Such indecisiveness and overcaution may be regarded as the opposite of jerking. Moreover, holding too long stems from the lack of coordination of movement which frequently occurs during those stages of training when the process of inhibition outweighs the process of stimulation. Simply stated, the shooter cannot force himself to exert positive pressure on the trigger at the proper time. One favorable moment after another goes past, and soon the chances for an accurate shot are gone. Naturally, the trigger control phase has been extended far beyond its effective duration. This situation frequently occurs after a period of dry-fire training exercises. The shooter loses the sense of the trigger's true weight when he fires for extended periods of time with a round in the chamber. When the trigger is released in a dry shot, the trigger seems to be rather light, but when the shooter switches to live rounds, the trigger weight seems to be considerably greater. He feels that he must exert greater effort to overcome this seemingly greater weight. Frequently, the shooter will blame his troubles on faulty adjustment of the trigger mechanism. Nothing is gained from such assumptions. More times than not, the shooter returns to normal trigger control since the root of the evil is lack of coordinated control and not trigger adjustment.

c. The restoration of coordination of movement, and the return to the correct balance between stimulation and inhibition is brought about primarily through systematic practice, match training and dry-fire exercises. It is precisely this method of training which develops the necessary coordination of the shooter's actions. When the shooter's movements become automatic, the trigger finger will operate in an unstrained manner, and the shot will break at the proper moment. It is important that each training session begin with a few dry-fire exercises. It has been demonstrated that such exercises are necessary for the development of accurate shooting. Such exercises may also be repeated after record shooting to restore equilibrium in the nervous processes.

d. Frequently, a shooter, when firing for record, is unable to fire a shot. After several unsuccessful tries, a loss of confidence will arise. Rather than risk a wild shot the shooter should unload the pistol, time permitting, and dry-fire a few shots. After restoring coordination of movement and regaining his confidence, the shooter is far better prepared, both physically and mentally, for the delivery of an accurate shot. Firing the shot during the first few seconds after settling into a good hold will guarantee confidence.

3. We have considered the fundamental errors that arise in trigger control. Let us now consider a problem that is also closely related to trigger control - trigger adjustment.

a. The firing of an accurate shot depends to a great extent on the quality of the trigger adjustment. An incorrectly adjusted trigger aggravates the errors committed by the shooter as he exerts pressure on the trigger. Incorrect adjustments include:

(1) Excessive trigger weight.

(2) Excessive long creep (movement of trigger).

(3) Too light trigger weight.

(4) Variable trigger weight.

b. The shooter should not try to overcome these difficulties with modification in his trigger control but take the problem and pistol to the armorer (gunsmith) for solution.

SECTION TWO

EMPLOYMENT OF THE FUNDAMENTALS

CHAPTER IV

ESTABLISHING A SYSTEM

The requirement that 120-270 record shots be fired in one day of match shooting demands great expenditure of energy. For this reason the shooter must plan his actions with special care in order to use his energy intelligently and conserve his physical and mental strength for the duration of the shoot.

The best method in which the shooter can impart all of his shooting skill to his shooting is by careful organization of maximum control.

Most of the points lost in an aggregate score are slow fire points. It is therefore imperative that this stage of fire become the first goal of exact control. One shot in one minute is sufficient time to organize the delivery of each shot. Successful delivery is assured when control of the cycle of action and thought is uniformly established - prepare, plan, relax, deliver, analyze and correct.

A. PREPARATION

Complete preparation and prior planning is essential. The firer must be both mentally and physically ready. So that he can concentrate on performance he must have checked the range conditions, his equipment, zero of weapons, range commands, ammunition, etc. prior to actual participation on the line.

1. **Zeroing:**

As a competitive shooter you must know how to zero your weapon in order to place the strike of the bullet in the center of the target.

There is no excuse for losing points in competition due to an improperly zeroed pistol. Inexact zeroing is a demonstration of lack of preparation.

a. There are two types of sights, fixed and adjustable.

(1) You may have fired a pistol with fixed sights. It could be that you are using a pistol with fixed sights now. The fixed sights found on the .45 caliber service pistol are somewhat difficult to adjust and therefore not primarily used for competitive shooting. For elevation correction, you must use the trial and error method of changing the sight height with a file, or, if a good armorer is available, he will be able to cut off the exact amount from the sights. Windage must be corrected by moving the rear sight with either a sight mover or a hammer and punch. You cannot have both a 25 yard and 50 yard zero in elevation with fixed sights. Your point of aim at 50 yards will be higher than at 25 yards. Correcting for windage with a fixed sight is very difficult due to the method used. Except for initial determination of normal zero for ideal conditions, it is recommended that fixed sights not be moved during competition.

(2) Most pistols that are used in competition today are equipped with adjustable sights which are easily moved by a screwdriver or a small coin.

(a) There are many makes of adjustable sights available on the market today. The sight adjustment screws do not all move in the same direction for a given adjustment. Clockwise will move one sight to the right and move another sight to the left. This also applies to elevation adjustment. Another difference is that each sight does not move the strike of the bullet the same distance per click. Some of these sights are more durable than others.

(b) The primary consideration when you are using adjustable sights is that you know the capabilities of your sights. How far one click in elevation moves the strike of the bullet at 50 yards, etc., on your pistol, is important to correct zeroing and adjusting.

(1) We recommend that you start your zero at twenty-five yards. Fire at least three rounds slow fire before moving the sights.

(2) Check your group in relation to the center of the target and if necessary, make a bold sight change. Do not creep to the center of the target one click at a time. Also, repeat the shot group method to establish a 50 yard zero. Do not try to zero by moving your sights after you have fired only one round. One round can easily be off because of errors committed by the shooter.

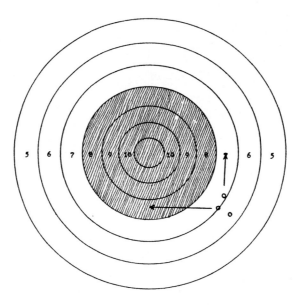

Figure 4-1. Sight Change Example.

The shot group is equivalent to an 8 ring or a four inch error at 6 o'clock in elevation. If the sight moves the strike of the bullet one-half inch per click at 50 yards - approximately eight clicks increase in elevation are needed. The group is equivalent to 7 ring or five and one-half inch error in windage at 3 o'clock, approximately eleven clicks of left windage are needed. (Refer to scoring ring dimensions in Sight Adjustment Card.)

(3) Exception to the shot group method may be made when a shooter with extensive experience is firing in a match and has called his shot good, but the shot was not located on the target in relation to his call. Analyze your shooting performance. You may determine that an immediate sight change is necessary, but do not be in too great a hurry to move your sights, as the chances for error caused by faulty technique are many.

(4) When the group is centered you may wish to fire 10 and 20 second strings to confirm the zero at 25 yards. There will possibly be a change required when shooting timed and rapid fire.

(5) Never "Hold Off" or use "Kentucky Windage" with adjustable sights. The shooter will force the shot to break at a specific spot instead of allowing the normal arc of movement. If you are grouping away from the center of the target, adjust the sights to compensate for the error. Mark and record your zero sight settings.

(a) It is a good idea to mark the sight adjustment screw with a small drop of nail polish or airplane dope to indicate the position of the 25 yard and 50 yard zero.

(b) You may also set the elevation screw down to its lowest point, counting the clicks as you do and record the number of clicks up from the bottom for both settings. This way you record the number of clicks from the base of the sight up to your 25 yard and 50 yard zero. (This method is used only for elevation.)

28

(c) You may also make a sight adjustment card on which you can record the zero position of the windage and elevation screw for all weapons. At certain times on different ranges, and under various weather and light conditions, you may find your zero changes slightly. (Figure 4-2).

Figure 4-2. Example of Sight Adjustment Card.

(6) A scorebook which has provisions for you to write in your sight settings for specific ranges, light and weather condition, and hard to remember data is a necessary item of equipment (Figure 4-4). Unusual zero changes frequently appear without reason. Some things to check are as follows:

(a) Check the spotting telescope: You may be scoping the adjacent target. Adjusting your zero to compensate for another shooter's grouping frequently happens.

(b) Check front and rear sights. The sights may have become loosened from the recoil or bent or damaged. The rear sight may have worn notches in the adjustments and would allow recoil to disturb the sight setting or when an adjustment is attempted, the sight would not move in the desired direction.

(c) Errors in position and grip may cause the hold and sight alignment to drift even though the shooter may have made a correction. An artificial correction is made to compensate for errors. At the shoulder it affects the hold, and at the wrist it affects the grip. An integral shift in body position should be made by moving the rear foot in the direction of the error in the hold and the grip should be shifted by sliding the grasp of the hand on the grips of the weapon toward the error. If a natural position and grip are attained, the tendency to point at other than the aiming point will be removed.

(d) Positive action is urgently needed when any of the above situations are present. Make a quick check of the scope, position, and grip and then continue until it is apparent that the difficulty is not being remedied. A bold change in sight setting should now be made.

(e) In the case of a sight damaged beyond use, ask the range officer to permit you to declare the weapon disabled and change guns or have it repaired by a qualified gunsmith on the range.

(f) The scorebook may indicate a large change in sight adjustment for the pistol range on which you are firing. Changes in light angle or light intensity may affect the zero that you use on the home range.

(7) Upon completion of firing, a consultation with your gunsmith might uncover certain changes in the fitting of components, wear, burrs or foreign matter that can alter the mating of finely fitted parts. Any of these may cause a change in zero.

2. _Preparation in the Assembly Area_: Before you can employ a systematic technique of shooting, a systematic preparation phase must be established. Actually the shooter's over-all preparation

starts the first time he attempts to improve his shooting ability. However, important steps can be taken during the period immediately before shooting that will favorably affect control and coordination.

a. Physical: The shooter must first complete his preparation in order to fully concentrate on shot delivery. The important thing to remember is to perform all operations and checks before record firing. Otherwise, the shooter will have to alter his system of control to compensate for the time lost in searching for an emergency solution.

(1) A shooter should eat light but nourishing food so that there will be no feeling of hunger before shooting, or a sensation of being stuffed. Avoid drinking a lot of water before and especially during shooting. Heavy food and too much liquid raises the pulse beat and induces excessive perspiration, thus weakening the body during shooting.

(2) Before shooting the shooter should do mild limbering up exercises: static tension exercises, walking, dry firing, etc., will revive blood circulation after sleep and help balance the nervous system. If a shooter starts shooting shortly after awakening, without limbering up, he will not be steady. His reactions are too slow, and his movements will lack coordination.

(3) The shooter should report to the range at least 15-30 minutes prior to firing time. This is necessary for equipment preparation and the shooter will also have a chance to relax and become settled during this period. Carrying a heavy gun box puts a strain on the shooter and no effort should be made to shoot for a period after such exertion.

(4) Checking the firing point from which a competitor will shoot must be given due attention.

(a) The shooter must choose the best place to shoot from. On a bright day, for example, the position should be slightly back, to allow shooting from shadow if possible, or he must place himself to the rear of his gun kit so as to be in its shadow. Establish your position in such a way that it will not be necessary to change once the shooting begins. Shooting glasses to prevent the sun from shining into the eyes should always be used.

(b) Frequently, the surface of the firing line has bumps, slopes, and other irregularities in it. In order that there be no unevenness on the firing line to interfere with a proper position, a shooter should level his area, scraping smooth the bumps or filling in the depressions with loose dirt or gravel before shooting starts.

(5) Before arriving at the firing line a shooter must have previously inspected his clothing and shoes carefully for comfortable fit.

(6) Before your relay is called you should move your equipment to a location directly behind your firing point. Make a final check to be sure you have the proper weapon, magazines and ammunition. Blacken your sights with the carbide lamp and make sure the sight setting is correct. Clean your shooting glasses, check for a pencil, screw driver, ear plugs and stop watch. Listen to the range commands and observe the range operation. Be aware of conditions and adapt your performance to take advantage of knowing beforehand the conditions under which you will have to fire. For example: Check for rapidly spoken fire commands, evaluate the wind and light by observing the effect on previous relays, etc. As soon as you are satisfied that you are familiar with the range and range operation, you should mentally review each step you must go through in delivering a good shot.

b. Mental: At the beginning of a shooting day it is a good idea to concentrate on planning each shot as a prelude to actual firing. Experienced shooters as a rule, take into account their feelings, energy and fitness and plan a definite method for themselves.

(1) Stimulate your confidence by developing a conviction that a controlled, uniform and exacting performance will produce good scores. Accept scores that are within your ability to hold. Confidence is a deciding factor. You will achieve a flawless performance if you are convinced you are capable of winning the match.

(2) Prior planning of your actions in the delivery of each shot will minimize the destructive effect of tension and pressure.

(3) Delay and irregularities in range operation upset some shooters. Remain relaxed and exercise patience.

(4) When you are shooting, you must think shooting, and only shooting. Be mentally alert and remove all stray thoughts from your mind. Condition your mind to concentrate on the match.

(5) Mentally review the entire shot sequence, with emphasis on how you are going to perform each act.

3. <u>Preparation on the firing line</u>: Having made sure that we are prepared to shoot the match, the shooter sets up his gun box and scope and makes a final check of his weapon, equipment, and of himself. (Refer to "Three Minute Preparation On The Firing Line Checklist" Figure 4-3).

a. Check your squadding ticket and place your shooting box on the correct firing point. This eliminates the unnecessary shuffle when another competitor informs you that you are on his firing point. Make sure you are correct and let him do the walking.

b. Set your scope on your target.

c. Scope your target and inspect for holes. Notify range operating personnel if the target is not ready for firing.

d. Adjust ear protectors.

e. Load magazines with proper caliber ammunition.

f. Make a final check of your weapon to see that the sights are still blackened. If the blacking has been rubbed off, then reblacken at this time.

g. Place all of your accessory shooting equipment that is located in the gun box on the shooting bench where it will be immediately available.

h. Most top shooters use approximately three minutes to carefully check out stance, position, and grip. Simultaneously, with this checking process, the shooter should be very careful not to shorten the depth of his breathing and at the end of the preparation sequence, should breathe deeply two or three times.

4. <u>Preparations after the command "LOAD" has been given.</u>

a. Upon the command to "LOAD," assume the stance, position and grip that you *previously* checked out to be correct. Verify this by extending the arm to check for a natural center hold and sight alignment with the target.

b. Load your weapon: Pay particular attention to see that the magazine catch has engaged the magazine. Failure of the weapon to load, caused by the magazine being partially placed in the weapon is not a valid reason for an alibi.

c. Keep the weapon pointed downrange.

d. With the non-shooting hand, grasp the weapon by the barrel or slide. Recheck for a good comfortable grip on the weapon. Check the position of your trigger finger. Extend the shooting arm briefly again to check if the hold and sight alignment are naturally obtained.

e. Check again that you are lined up on proper target.

f. Relax with the pistol muzzle touching the bench.

g. Continue the mental process, knowing that you are prepared to do the job. Mentally review the sequence of events necessary to deliver a correct shot or string. Concentrate on shot sequence. Visualize perfect sight alignment.

A checklist that can be stapled inside the lid of your gun box is recommended for use during all preparation.

ASSEMBLY AREA PREPARATION	FIRING LINE 3 MINUTE PREPARATION
(a) Check Squadding for Relay and Target. (b) Have the Proper Gun & Ammunition. (c) Check the Sight Settings. (d) Carbide Light WITH CARBIDE. (e) Blacken the Sights. (f) Position Ear Plugs or Protectors. (g) Oil Can - check Lubrication. (h) Screw Driver for Sight Change. (i) Stop Watch for Timing. (j) Scorebook. BE READY For Relay to be Called. Look to the Weather. Time Range Commands. Concentrate on Fundamentals. Rehearse Mentally.	DO NOT HANDLE Weapons Until the Range Officer Gives Clearance to do so. (a) Set Up Scope ON TARGET. (b) Check Target For Holes. (c) Adjust Ear Plugs. (d) Load Magazines. (e) Recheck Sight Blackening. (f) Check Grip & Position. (g) Locate all Shooting Equipment. (h) Breath Control. RELAX PHYSICALLY Continue Mental Processing THINK POSITIVELY Act Aggressively YOU - ARE - READY!!!

Figure 4-3. Preparation Checklist.

5. <u>The items that are important aids to the shooter</u> should be present and operative prior to shooting.

a. Carbide Lamp with Carbide: This small item may be termed one of the most important accessories in the shooter's kit. But it does not work without carbide. Be sure the lamp is ready and spare flints and carbide are on hand.

b. Magazine: Extra magazines are necessary to insure continuous operation. Be sure they are clean, operative and on hand in the gun box.

c. Ammunition: Have the correct amount and caliber of ammunition for the match being fired. Include enough for refires due to malfunctions, range alibis, etc.

d. Pencil and Score Book: Have a pencil or pen on hand. In some matches you will be called upon to score. Your scorebook should always be kept up to date whether in practice or in a match.

e. Ear Plugs: Protect your ears at all times from possible damage and eliminate breaks in concentration by closing out gun blast and extraneous sounds by use of ear protection.

f. Glasses with Cleaning Tissue: Colored lenses afford glare protection and are designed to let in only glare-free light. Corrective, plain or colored glasses also protect the eyes from possible damage from ejected shells, etc., and should be worn at all times when on the line. Use them to best advantage by keeping them clean. Have lens tissues in your kit.

g. Screwdriver and Tools: Sights were made to be moved. Tools that will prove useful are: cleaning rod, barrel bushing wrench, allen wrench set, and screwdrivers. Be sure they are all on hand.

h. Weapons and Magazines: A properly cleaned and lubricated weapon will have much less chance of malfunctioning. Look and see if you have clean magazines for the correct weapons.

i. Squadding Tickets: It is best to rely on your squadding ticket to inform you of your firing point and correct relay. Do not rely on memory. Keep them on your person or in your gun box at all times.

j. Stop Watch: A stop watch is an efficient means to pace your shooting during slow nre.

k. Sight Setting: Check to see if you have the sights set for the range at which this match will be fired.

l. Lubrication: Have a can of light machine oil available.

As a student of advanced pistol marksmanship, there should never arise any circumstances under which the results of your efforts are jeopardized by your failure to make complete and painstaking prep aration.

B. PLAN SHOT SEQUENCE

There must be a systematic approach to obtaining shooting control. To successfully employ the fundamentals the shooter must develop a plan of action and fix it so firmly in mind that distractions do not interfere with his ability to follow a planned sequence. Simply giving yourself the order to watch the sights, hold, and squeez is not sufficient.

A shooter with natural talent may find it possible to occasionally fire good strings without having a plan of action. But regardless of his talent his performance is going to be erratic until he uses a comprehensive plan.

The shooter must realize that his ability to consistently perform well under pressure is related to the uniformity of his preparation. A planned sequence of thinking that will guide his physical actions through the complete string of fire is absolutely necessary.

You must control your mind and stop disconcerting thoughts of the possibility of failure. Picture yourself as you felt and thought while firing good strings and then ask yourself what technique you were using that enabled you to employ the fundamentals so successfully. The difference between champions and the also-rans lies in the ability to control thinking and plan actions from this point on. Prior planning of the delivery of the shot is the shooter's only insurance that the delivery will be consistently controlled. Knowledge of a successful shot sequence is the basis of the plan. The best assurance that a good performance can be duplicated is that the action follow a uniform sequence.

1. Remind yourself that when you consistently controlled your shooting you were using a shot sequence. You proved that there is a shot sequence that will work successfully for you. You must recreate precisely those same conditions to get the same results.

The course of fire may have a successful conclusion only if the shooter, in setting-up each shot, goes through all the stages - getting completely ready, planning, relaxing, and delivering the shot, analyzing and correcting in the same manner each time.

2. The following sequence is recommended for slow fire:

a. Extend arm and breathe.

b. Settle into a minimum arc of movement.

c. Pick up sight alignment in the aiming area.

d. Take up trigger slack - apply initial pressure.

e. Hold breath.

f. Maintain sight alignment and minimum arc of movement.

g. Start positive trigger pressure.

h. Concentrate point focus on front sight.

i. Follow through. (Occurs with surprise shot only) (No reflex action)

33

3. The following sequence is recommended for timed and rapid:

    a. Extend shooting arm and breathe.

    b. Find sight alignment.

    c. Find aiming area on edge of target frame (final deep breath).

    d. Settle into minimum arc of movement.

    e. Point focus of front sight (Partly release breath).

    f. Take up slack - apply initial trigger pressure.

    g. Maintain sight alignment (target faces).

    h. Start positive trigger pressure.

    i. Concentrate on sight alignment (first shot is fired).

4. When a shooter has a system to follow, he can concentrate on performance and not be worried about results. Care should be taken during early stages of instructional practice to comply with each of the items on the shooter's worksheet. As the shooter becomes more capable, sequence, analysis and corrective action becomes more important. Repetition of these steps will instill in the shooter good habits that will enable him to repeat good performance. Further, the worksheet will help the shooter form the habit of not overlooking any factor that will help his shooting. Winning scores are produced by being ready, confident, performing uniformly and being in complete control.

C. RELAXATION

1. Relaxation is best achieved by methodically bringing about a loosening of the muscular masses of the body. Think of the neck muscles, the shoulder, back, abdomen, buttocks and upper legs. Systematically reduce the tension of these members to one of support of an upright stance only.

2. A relaxed muscle does not become as tired as quickly as a tense one. It is also important to rest and relax after two or three shots during slow fire.

D. DELIVER SHOT OR STRING OF SHOTS ON TARGET

The successful delivery of an accurate shot on the target, embraces the proper employment of all the fundamentals. Do not compromise. Follow through and continue to apply all control factors. If the shot is fired as a surprise, there will be no reflex action. When you are absolutely sure you have set up conditions for a controlled shot, put your plan into action. Convidently and aggressively follow each mental step with physical action until the sequence is complete and the shot is delivered on the target.

Remember that in slow fire you do not have to shoot before bringing your gun down to rest. When you fatigue, run short of breath, experience difficulty in maintaining concentration on sight alignment or cannot maintain a suitable arc of movement, lower the weapon to the bench and relax. Replan the delivery of the shot, breathe deeply and try again. Some excellent slow fire shooters try two or three times before being able to deliver a controlled shot. Full control of the application of the fundamentals insures the correct control of a shot.

1. Example of a system delivering rapid fire strings with fire commands: As the Range Officer starts his commands, he will announce:

    a. "ON THE FIRING LINE, FOR YOUR FIRST STRING OF RAPID FIRE. WITH FIVE ROUNDS LOAD."

    (1) You should load at this time and assume your grip.

    b. "IS THE LINE READY?"

(1) Continue your rhythmic breathing.

(2) Check that you are going to shoot on the proper target.

c. "READY ON THE RIGHT."

(1) Extend the arm with a stiff wrist and a locked elbow.

(2) Align the sights.

(3) Breathe deeply and exhale.

d. "READY ON THE LEFT."

(1) Find the aiming area on the edge of the target frame.

(2) Take a final deep breath.

(3) Settle into a minimum arc of movement.

e. "READY ON THE FIRING LINE."

(1) Partly release the breath and hold the remainder.

(2) Point of focus is on the front sight.

(3) Take up the slack - apply initial trigger pressure.

(4) Maintain sight alignment.

f. Target faces toward shooter - commence firing.

(1) Start positive trigger pressure.

(2) Shift concentration to perfecting sight alignment.

g. First shot is fired (Surprise Shot).

(1) Maintain eye focus (follow through).

(2) Quick recovery with the sights approximately in alignment, and hold approximately in center of aiming area.

(3) Renew positive trigger pressure.

(4) Strive to correct errors in sight alignment, but do not delay positive trigger pressure.

h. Follow through with four more surprise shots.

i. Good rhythm indicates coordinated application of the fundamentals.

E. MAKE AN ANALYSIS

Complete and instantaneous shot analysis is a prerequisite for improvement in performance or score. It is a complete waste of time and ammunition to fire haphazardly without any comprehensive attempt to improve. A mental impression of the sight alignment should come at the instant the shot breaks.

It is advantageous to analyze why you are shooting well on a particular day. Some shooters have a tendency to ignore their good scores. It is important to analyze the good shot string so the combination of factors that produce these good strings can be remembered and repeated. In making the analysis, an important point to remember is to be honest with yourself and your coach. By admitting mistakes the shooter can correct them. The coach can help find a solution to mistakes which he was not aware of if you reveal everything you saw, heard or thought of during the firing of the shot or string.

If any shooter critically re-examines and analyzes his performance and his technique of shooting, he will find "minor points," which to a certain extent hinder him from improving his results. The elimination of individual shortcomings and poor methods are the method the shooter has at his disposal to increase his competitive stature.

    1. <u>Slow Fire</u>:

    a. Steps:

    (1) Call each shot. Base your call primarily on the relationship of the front and rear sight. Also consider any unusual occurrences in the arc of movement and whether or not concentration on sight alignment was maintained.

    (2) When you have decided where your shot should be located on the target, verify your call by observation with the spotting scope.

    (3) If the shot or call is good or bad, determine the cause. Generally one of the following situations will occur:

    (a) Shot call and shot location coincide and you have a good shot.

    (b) Shot call and shot location coincide, but shot is bad.

    (c) Shot call and shot location do not coincide.

NOTE: ANY TIME YOU FAIL TO RECOGNIZE THE ERROR, YOU MUST EXAMINE YOUR PLAN TO MAKE SURE YOU HAVE NOT NEGLECTED A FUNDAMENTAL.

    (4) Evaluation: Now consider the question - Did you or did you not follow the planned sequence? If your answer is yes and you had an acceptable shot, this should stimulate your confidence. Review the technique you used to deliver the successful shot. Make every effort to reestablish the same conditions that existed for the first controlled shot and repeat the sequence for each succeeding shot. If your answer was no, you must identify the specific point in your shot sequence where control was lost. The following examples cover only a few of the errors that may have occurred:

    (a) Failure to establish a minimum arc of movement.

    (b) Inability to maintain point focus on sight alignment.

    (c) Concentration drifts from sight alignment to trigger control.

    (d) Trigger pressure intermittent and uncertain with considerable effort required to fire the pistol.

    (e) Lack of aggressive, determined attitude, and confidence in the technique.

    b. The shooter's slow fire work sheet lists the following steps as a guide to complete shot analysis:

    (1) Follow through check.

    (2) Call shot (describe sight alignment).

    (3) Compare target hit location with shot call.

    (4) If shot or call is bad, determine cause.

(5) Watch for error pattern to form. (Same error on more than one shot)

(6) Did shot break in normal arc of movement?

(7) Did you hold too long?

(8) Did you apply positive trigger pressure?

(9) If you benched weapon on a shot effort, why?

(10) Did you lose concentration? (What did you think about other than sight alignment?)

(11) Did you get a surprise shot break?

(12) Were you worried about results?

2. Strings of Five Shots:

After each five shot string, the shooter should remember each shot as one of five individual sight alignments that enables him to accurately call the shot group. If the call and the group are not together it is necessary to determine the cause and apply positive correction. If the group is not centered then the weapon isn't zeroed, the position was bad or the grip incorrect. If the shooter is sure of the zero of his weapon, then quickly check out the position and grip before firing the next five shot string. Look for one of the five following situations to occur. (It is possible however, for two or more of the situations to occur in one string.)

a. Shots off call and grouped within ability to hold, but not centered on target.

b. Shots on call but group larger than normal holding ability and may or may not be centered on target.

c. Shots off call, group larger than holding ability and may or may not be centered on target.

d. Shots on call grouped within ability to hold, but off center on target.

e. The shooter's rapid fire worksheet lists the following steps as a guide to complete shot group analysis:

(1) Follow through the proper recovery checkout.

(2) Shot group call (describe five individual sight alignments).

(3) Compare group location with call.

(4) If shot group or call is bad, determine cause.

(5) Did you get a surprise break on each of five shots?

(6) Was the first shot fired on time?

(7) Was rhythm maintained throughout string including last shot?

(8) Did all shots break in normal arc of movement?

(9) Did you apply positive trigger pressure on each of five shots?

(10) Did you lose concentration during string? (What were you thinking of)?

(11) Did you ignore minor errors in hold?

(12) Were you worried about results?

F. POSITIVE CORRECTION (If Necessary)

1. After a shot analysis, corrective measures have to be incorporated into the shooter's performance if the error is to be avoided on the next shot. Slipshod analysis, if any, is usually compounded by the absence of corrective action. Without analysis and corrective measure, improvement is at an end. The shooter who has not learned what he is doing wrong, or what to do about it if the trouble is found is lost and will never excel.

2. Corrective measures prevent the recurrence of poor performance and must be immediately applied. Much has been written about why we shoot poorly; however, it is just as advantageous to analyze why you are shooting well on a particular day. It is more helpful to know the right way to perform than to have your mind cluttered with a multitude of "don't." Coaches in particular should concentrate on and emphasize the positive factors.

3. Look for, analyze and correct mistakes every time a shot is fired.

4. There must be agreement on corrective measures between coach and shooter. The coach must explain the reasons for specific corrective measures recommended.

G. USING ADDITIONAL AIDS TO ORGANIZE A SYSTEM OF SHOOTING

1. The sight adjustment card furnishes information on sight capabilities, aids in obtaining a zero and provides a convenient record of sight settings for all caliber weapons.

2. The preparation check sheet provides a convenient list of actions necessary to shoot successfully.

3. The pistol scorebook: The pistol scorebook is a valuable aid to the competitive pistol shooter. It is an individual shooter's record of all firing by stage, such as slow, timed, and rapid fire, plus National Match Course and the value of all shots fired should be recorded. Practice scores should be kept separate from Match Scores.

The score book is valuable only if it is kept accurately and up to date. Record the bad scores as well as the good ones. By keeping the scorebook accurately it will be an aid in finding weak points in the shooter's performance. The scorebook will show over a period of time a trend in the shooter's progress. It will reflect progress in the different stages of fire. Averages may also be kept in the scorebook for each stage of fire. Record of ammunition used, sight adjustment, windage, and elevation, weather, light, wind, temperature, may be an aid to the shooter at a later day. There are many type scorebooks that will do the job well, but choose the one that is simple and will furnish the data you need quickly. An example of pistol scorebook page appears on the following page.

4. Due to the great number of functions necessary for the shooter to apply in exercising control of his shooting, a worksheet for both slow and rapid fire is furnished.

a. The slow fire worksheet provides the shooter with a guide to organization and application of a system for the control of a slow fire shot.

b. The timed and rapid fire worksheet provides the shooter with a guide to the organization and application of a system for the control of a five shot string of timed or rapid fire.

DATE				LOCATION						TOTAL		AMMO CALIBER						WIND		LIGHT		
1	2	3	4	5	6	7	8	9	10	TOTAL		1	2	3	4	5	6	7	8	9	10	TOTAL
											SL											
											TM											
ELEV		WIND		SF TOTAL							RP											
1	2	3	4	5	6	7	8	9	10			NMC TOTAL										
												TOTAL AGGREGATE										
												NMC TEAM MATCH										
ELEV		WIND		TF TOTAL								1	2	3	4	5	6	7	8	9	10	TOTAL
1	2	3	4	5	6	7	8	9	10		SL											
											TM											
											RP											
ELEV		WIND		RF TOTAL								NMC TOTAL										

Figure 4-4. Example of the Pistol Scorebook Page.

H. ORGANIZED TRAINING

The champion shooter must be capable of intense concentration and have the sheer guts and determination to adhere to the application of fundamentals in spite of match pressure, adverse weather conditions, discouragement, gun trouble and possible sickness. The best method of sustaining good performance is good organization. To shoot well, do more of the little things right. If you are well organized, overall superiority will result. The knowledge of a systematic approach to controlled shooting must be thoroughly ingrained in the minds of all shooters. The "edge" lies with the shooter with a system.

It should be added that any system will be worthless to a shooter who has indifferent attitudes toward training and who turns the training sessions into a fixed routine, repeating in robot-like fashion the prescribed shooting aspects of a competitive shooter's activity. It requires not only systematic and painstaking work, but a thoughtful analysis of his work, continuous striving for the new and better, a bold search for the best, and an unwavering strengthening of his will. Only such work on his own shooting methods will turn a shooter's training into a reliable means of assuring his further development and make it possible for him to win.

SLOW FIRE WORKSHEET

PREPARATORY (In assembly area)

1. Squadding-Proper Relay & Target
2. Using clean weapons - Proper Caliber
3. Proper sight setting (Zeroed)
4. Blacken sights
5. Ammunition, Ear Plugs & Screwdriver

PREPARATORY (On firing line)

6. Focus scope on proper target
7. Dry Fire for natural Position & Grip
8. Adjust ear plugs
9. Ammunition loaded into magazine
10. Mental Stimulation of Confidence

PLAN DELIVERY OF SHOT (Review Shot Sequence)

11. Extend arm & breathe deeply
12. Settle into minimum arc of movement
13. Pick up sight alignment in aiming area
14. Take up trigger slack - apply initial pressure
    (take final breath and hold part of it)
15. Maintain sight alignment and minimum arc of movement
16. Start positive trigger pressure
17. Concentrate point focus on front sight

RELAXATION

18. No unnecessary muscular tension
    (Relax each major portion of body)

DELIVER SHOT (Follow Plan - No Compromise)

19. Follow Through (Continue all control factors)
20. Shot fired as a surprise - No reflex action

SHOT ANALYSIS

21. Call Shot - describe sight alignment
22. Compare hit location with call
23. If shot or call is bad, determine cause
24. Watch for formation of error pattern
25. Did shot break in minimum arc of movement?
26. Hold too long?
27. Positive trigger pressure?
28. Benched weapon, why?
29. Lost concentration?
30. Surprise shot break?
31. Worried about results?

POSITIVE CORRECTION (Prompt Application)

32. Include in plan of delivery of next shot.

Figure 4-5. Slow Fire Worksheet.

RAPID FIRE WORKSHEET

	1	2	3	4

PREPARATORY (In assembly area)

1. Squadding - Proper Relay and Target

2. Using clean weapons - Proper Caliber

3. Proper sight setting (Zeroed)

4. Blacken Sights

5. Ammunition, Ear Plugs & Screwdriver

PREPARATORY (On Firing Line)

6. Focus scope on proper target

7. Dry fire for natural position & grip

8. Adjust ear plugs

9. Ammunition loaded into magazine

10. Mental Stimulation of Confidence

PLAN DELIVERY OF STRING (Review Sequence)

11. Extend arm & breathe deeply

12. Find sight alignment

13. Find aiming area on edge of target frame
    (Final deep breath)

14. Settle into minimum arc of movement

15. Point focus on front sight (partly release breath)

16. Take up slack - Initial pressure

17. Maintain sight alignment & minimum arc of movement
    (Target faces)

18. Start positive trigger pressure

19. Concentrate on sight alignment
    (First shot is fired)

RELAXATION

20. No Unnecessary Muscular Tension
    (Relax each major portion of body)

DELIVER STRING OF FIVE SHOTS

21. Follow through and recover with good sight alignment
    and central hold on each shot of string

SHOT GROUP ANALYSIS

22. Group call. Describe five individual sight alignments

23. Compare group location with calls

24. If group or call is bad, determine cause

25. Surprise break on each of five shots?

26. First shot on time & rhythm maintained?

27. Did shots break in minimum arc of movement?

28. Positive trigger pressure?

29. Lost concentration?

30. Ignored minor errors?

31. Worried about results?

POSITIVE CORRECTION (Prompt Application)

32. Include in plan of delivery of next five shots.

Figure 4-6. Rapid Fire Worksheet.

AN OUTLINE SUMMARY OF THE COMPLETE SEQUENCE OF FIRING ONE ACCURATE SHOT

1. Preparation: In assembly area and on firing line
   a. Physical
      (1) Personal preparation.
      (2) Limbering up. Arrive early.
      (3) Check out firing line.
         (a) Protection from wind and bright or changing sunlight.
         (b) Smooth and even horizontal surface.
      (4) Fit of clothing and shoes (boots)
      (5) Make final check in assembly area of all necessary equipment and become aware of firing conditions both weatherwise and in range operation.
      (6) Move to firing line and place equipment on your firing point.
      (7) Set telescope up on your target.
      (8) Make final check of weapon. Check sight black. Should be Zeroed.
      (9) Check for proper caliber and amount of ammunition and load magazines.
      (10) Check out stance and position for natural pointing at target center.
      (11) Check out grip for natural alignment of sight when incorporating all requirements of a good grip.
      (12) Breathe Deeply for increased oxygen retention.
   b. Mental
      (1) Stimulate confidence.
      (2) Think only of shooting and expel all stray thoughts.
      (3) Let the coach worry about any distractions or interruptions on the firing line.
      (4) Mentally review shot sequence:
         (a) Think of the act of extending arm and breathing deeply.
         (b) Think of how your minimum arc of movement looks and feels.
         (c) Picture properly aligned sights with point focus on front sight.
         (d) Decide at what point in sequence you are going to take up slack in trigger and apply initial pressure.
         (e) Here you take final deep breath, exhale and hold only part of it.
         (f) Remind yourself to maintain sight alignment and a minimum arc of movement while;
         (g) Positive, uninterrupted trigger pressure is being applied,
         (h) Concentration must shift to and remain unbroken on sight alignment while positive trigger pressure is being applied.
         (i) The pistol will seem to almost fire itself because positive trigger pressure is almost involuntary.
         (j) The surprise shot is now a possibility because with the employment of positive trigger pressure, the normal reaction time suffices to delay anticipatory reflexes that could disturb sight alignment, until all the continuously applied control factors can bring about the delivery of the shot on the target. This is, in effect, follow through.

2. Plan the Shot
   a. Stance
      (1) Stable balance.
      (2) Immobility.
      (3) Head position.
      (4) Uniformity.
      (5) Position of feet.
      (6) Body erect.
      (7) Shoulders level.
      (8) Legs firmly straight.
      (9) Hips level.
      (10) Head level.
      (11) Rest not-shooting arm and hand.
      (12) Solid firm shooting arm and hand.
      (13) Center of gravity slightly forward.
   b. Natural Position Orientation.
      (1) Start at 45 degree angle.
      (2) Turn only head to target.
      (3) Extend arm.
      (4) Close eyes.
      (5) Raise arm and settle.
      (6) Open eyes.
      (7) Shift trail foot in direction of error if necessary.
      (8) Recheck.
   c. Grip.
      (1) Natural sight alignment.
      (2) Firm to prevent shift.
      (3) Unchanging tightness.
      (4) Independent trigger finger.
      (5) Uniformity.
      (6) Comfortable.
      (7) Recoil straight to rear.
      (8) Avoid fatigue of hand.
   d. Breath Control.
      (1) Systematic.
      (2) Oxygen retention.
      (3) Minimize movement.
      (4) Respiratory pause.
      (5) Comfortable.
      (6) Concentration aided.
      (7) Prior to and during fire commands.
   e. Sight Alignment (Relationship of Front and Rear Sights not Sights to Target).
      (1) Front sight point focus.
      (2) Rear sight awareness.
      (3) Exclusive concentration.
      (4) 6 to 8 Seconds Duration.
      (5) Coordination with other control factors.
   f. Trigger Control.
      (1) Positive uninterrupted trigger pressure.
      (2) 2 to 5 second duration.
      (3) Based on perfect sight alignment.
      (4) Undisturbed sight alignment.
      (5) Coordinate with optimum perception, and minimum arc of movement.
   g. Shot Sequence.
      (1) Extend arm and breathe.
      (2) Settle into minimum arc of movement.
      (3) Pick up sight alignment in the aiming area.
      (4) Take up trigger slack and apply initial pressure.
      (5) Take final breath and hold part of it.
      (6) Maintain sight alignment and minimum arc of movement.
      (7) Start positive uninterrupted trigger pressure.
      (8) Concentrate point of focus on front sight.

3. Relaxation
   a. No unnecessary muscular tension.
   b. Relax each major portion of body:
      (1) Neck
      (2) Shoulders
      (3) Non-shooting arm
      (4) Abdomen
      (5) Back
      (6) Buttocks
      (7) Upper legs.

4. Deliver Shot
   a. As planned - Do not compromise. Apply all control factors.
   b. Follow through - continue to apply all control factors.
   c. Shot will fire as a surprise - no reflex action.

5. Shot Analysis
   (Use a target center to plot shot calls)
   a. Follow through check.
   b. Call shot - Describe sight alignment.
   c. Compare hit location with call.
   d. If shot or call is bad, determine cause.
   e. Watch for error pattern to form.
   f. If analysis is vague or unsure, ask yourself some or all of the following questions:
      (1) Did shot break in minimum arc of movement?
      (2) Hold too long?
      (3) Positive trigger pressure?
      (4) If shot could not be fired & shooter benched weapon, what was wrong?
      (5) Lost concentration?
      (6) Surprise shot break?
      (7) Worried about results?

6. Positive Correction, (If Necessary)
   a. Promptly applied,
   b. Agreement between coach and shooter,
   c. Incorporate into plan for next shot.

Figure 4-7. The Complete Sequence of Firing an Accurate Shot.

CHAPTER V

TECHNIQUE OF SLOW FIRE

A. GENERAL.

    1. A technique is the method of performing the procedures of an operation.

    2. A technique of slow fire that will permit a pistol shooter to compete successfully will include:

        a. Painstaking preparation.

        b. Thorough planning.

        c. Systematic relaxation of muscular system.

        d. Intense concentration.

        e. Coordination of all the fundamental factors in delivery of an accurate shot.

        f. Analysis of shot delivery.

        g. Correction of errors.

        h. Strict uniformity of execution of the above is required to insure duplication of a good performance time after time.

    3. The factors regarding the technique of slow fire shooting should not be regarded as hard and fast which demand strict execution of each point. In competitive shooting, as in any other sport, there are no established rules on technique that apply to all persons.

    4. The shooter should accept the material in this chapter in a critical manner, using it as a guide in finding his own style of shooting - a style that fits his temperament, individual ability and physical construction.

B. TECHNIQUES IN SLOW FIRE CONTROL.

    The best technique of control is slow fire, for each individual shooter, is the proper employment of a combination of the fundamental factors that contribute toward attaining satisfactory performance.

    1. Dry Firing Before Shooting: A shooter should rarely shoot the first time he settles to aim. Form the habit of firing a "dry" shot or two before the first shot. This will aid in attaining the sharp, clear focus necessary for a smooth, coordinated performance. Avoid dragging out a shot which results in increasing the arc of movement and dulling of the vision. A shooter, after trying unsuccessfully for five or six seconds, should stop dryfiring, take his finger from the trigger and rest, and then make another attempt to dry fire a satisfactory shot. Do not do this too many times, however. A long day's shooting will make heavy demands on the muscles and eyes.

    2. Carefulness: Great care is one of the mainstays of the control of slow fire shooting. Every shooter will get a certain percentage of good shots, the rest will be mediocre to poor. The poor shots result from carelessness. Accepting conditions as almost good enough is a form of carelessness. There are few top shooters who are absolutely without some compromise. The shooter who is not willing to devote himself fully and fails to pick up the tie breaking point is the one that loses the match. The principal damage that carelessness inflicts on controlled performance, strikes at the point where it can be least afforded; uniformity. For example, the failure to properly regrip the pistol for each new attempt to shoot, violates the stipulation that if a good performance is to be repeated, you must uniformly duplicate the employment of all the fundamentals.

3. Patience: Patience is of great importance to the conduct of slow fire, in that without it, the shooter may disrupt an otherwise good performance an instant from successful completion. When the conditions for a controlled, accurate shot are met, the problem facing the shooter is reduced to one of patiently allowing proposed events to follow their normal course. The syncronization of the factors in delivering an accurate shot require a certain time for completion. Any impatience that would cause one control factor to be disrupted will reduce the whole to a shambles. Improvised, desperate measures to reconstitute a lapse cannot possibly succeed. As an example, a shooter is on the firing line, making a concerted effort to maintain conditions that have been set up to control an accurate shot. His sights are aligned, the arc of movement is settling and he is positively pressing straight to the rear on the trigger, and then must momentarily wait. At this point in his technique of employing the fundamentals he will succeed or fail, depending upon his ability to allow the necessary time to pass for the smooth, undisturbed release of the hammer.

4. Over Sighting: A shooter must remember that his scores cannot be improved by sighting for a long time. On the contrary, "over-sighting" sharply reduces accuracy. After about ten or twelve seconds of sighting, vision becomes gradually blunted and the shooter's eye ceases to observe some minute errors. The result is a deceptive aim, and the shooter without noticing his error in sighting makes an inaccurate shot. In order to achieve the highest accuracy, sighting should be accomplished within six or eight seconds. This system of sighting is good because a shooter who does not over-sight and strain his eyes, permits them to recover rapidly and to keep their sharpness for the duration of the whole match.

5. Establishing a System: A system of operation must be devised by each shooter individually without which he is not capable of attaining a sustained high performance standard. Consult Chapter IV, "Establishing A System." The shooter's guide to comprehensive organization of control of a slow fire shot, "The Slow Fire Worksheet" is included in Chapter IV.

Completing the day's schedule of shooting successfully requires the shooter to go through all the stages of shooting for every shot in exactly the same way. This is possible only if the shooter can conserve sufficient physical energy, sharpness of vision, quickness of reaction, etc. while he is shooting. The ability to repeat everything the same way requires an intelligent and economic use of ones energies

6. The Tempo of Shooting: Experience has shown that the best way to shoot is to shoot each shot rapidly, within six seconds after settling. The time spent between each shot, preparing and planning, is limited only by the total time allowed for the stage of fire. All shooting should be done at a definite tempo and with a definite rhythm.

a. In order that the shooter not only expend his energies with care, but actually build them up during the course of shooting, adequate breaks should be taken both between shots and between series of shots. It is best to shoot at regular intervals, using all the time allotted for a particular match. In slow fire, circumstances rarely permit unbroken rhythmical shooting. Therefore, the shooter must take a particular situation and his own daily capabilities into account and shoot sometimes at an accelerated or reduced rate, thereby operating at a tempo that will permit maximum performance.

b. Before beginning to shoot for record, it is recommended the shooter fire "dry shots." If he feels that after the first shots that his shooting is going easily, he should proceed to shoot live ammo, making no attempt to slow down, so that the established coordination of his movements will not be upset.

c. When a shooter finds it difficult to shoot, he should not speed up his shooting. He must replan, relax, wait a short time until he has the "feel" of his pistol, shoot some "dry shots," patiently reestablish control of the trigger, aim with care before each shot, and then begin shooting with assurance at a quickened tempo in order to make up for lost time.

d. No matter how well the shooter is doing, a shooter should always be careful to control his movements at all times so as not to cause a performance failure because of negligence. There is no such thing as shooting for a long period of time without some loss of control. However, one must be constantly on guard against becoming nervous and rushing because of a bad shot, as if it is necessary to compensate in a short a time with good shooting for the poor shot. It usually happens that rushing leads to repetition of the same mistakes. Under such circumstances, analyze, correct errors, shoot without haste, and develop the next shot with more care.

e. The regular tempo of shooting applies when a shooter is shooting under favorable conditions in good shooting weather. If, on the other hand, the weather is not favorable, the shooter should use a different tempo and approach, depending on the conditions prevailing.

7. <u>Resting During the Breaks Between Shots</u>: During the rest period between shots, a shooter should see that uniformity in assuming body stance and positions is not destroyed. The angle at which the body is turned from the target and the relative position of the feet should not change. In order that the rest interval be most effective, it is a good idea to assume a posture which will make it possible for the muscles to relax and rebuild their strength. The best way is to put the pistol down on the table and sit down in a chair without moving the feet. You can mark the position of the feet with chalk if you are afraid the exact position of the feet cannot be duplicated. It is necessary, when shooting in gusty winds, to rest while standing, with the pistol in a slightly relaxed grip. The shooter must be prepared to assume the firing position quickly, to shoot between gusts, and during the best periods for firing.

D. COMMON POINTS OF DEFICIENCY IN CONTROL.

There are a multitude of causes for bad shots. Listed below are those most frequently found. It is not intended to be a complete list nor is it intended to provide the shooter with a convenient list of bad habits. It is, however, intended to assist the shooter in finding the source of his trouble.

1. <u>Jerk or Heel</u>: The abrupt application of pressure either with the trigger finger alone or in the case of heeling, pushing with the heel of the hand at the same time.

2. <u>Vacillation</u>: Lack of know-how and skill causes constant changing of technique. The end result is usually that you hope to get a good shot.

3. <u>Anxiety</u>: You work and work on a shot, meanwhile building up in your mind a doubt about being able to fire the shot while your control is optimum. Impatience sets in. Finally you shoot just to get rid of that particular round so you may work on others.

4. <u>Not Looking At the Sights</u>: This is listed frequently as "looking at the target." A shooter may be focusing his eye on neither the sights nor the target, but since he does not see the target in clear focus he assumes he is looking at the sights. Concentrate on sight alignment.

5. <u>Loss of Concentration</u>: The concentration will shift between sight alignment and the relative position of the sights to the target if good sight picture is the objective. Concentrate only on attaining perfect sight alignment with minimum movement and the application of positive trigger pressure comes much easier and is almost involuntary.

6. <u>Holding Too Long</u>: Adverse conditions that disturb a shooter's ability to "hold" will cause him to delay his positive application of trigger pressure while waiting for conditions to become better. The disturbing factor about this is that you will do it sometimes when you have your normal minimum arc of movement, therefore, you must try to freeze all arc of movement momentarily to get off a perfect shot quickly before any movement is resumed.

7. <u>Control</u>: Maintaining control of your shooting is a continuous battle. The battle builds tension. Tension tightens the muscles and finally the abrupt motions made in compensation for errors cause the shooter to go beyond the desired area and deliver shots in exactly the opposite place from where the error was causing him to shoot originally. Smooth coordinated actions are best assured by the relaxed, confident and carefully planned approach.

8. <u>Lack of Follow Through</u>: Follow through is the conscious attempt to keep all control factors applied through the break of the shot. For example, you are continuing to maintain concentration on sight alignment even after the shot is on the way. This is accomplished by having a surprise shot break and no reflexes of anticipation to disturb sight alignment. Follow through is not to be confused with recovery. Merely recovering from recoil and reestablishing the hold and sight alignment after the shot is fired is no indication that you are following through.

9. <u>Match Pressure</u>: (See Chapter VII - Mental Discipline) If there are 200 competitors in a match, rest assured that there are 200 shooters suffering from match pressure. You should exert all your mental energy toward planning and executing the fundamentals correctly.

E. WIND SHOOTING AND ADVERSE CONDITIONS.

In a shooting day the weather is apt to change drastically but not necessarily very often. This means that a shooter must be able to react to all changes taking place around him and to change his method of shooting accordingly.

A shooter should also be guided by the rule that shooting should not be rushed when the weather conditions are changing frequently. He should be particularly attentive and carefully analyze any weather condition. After making a decision to shoot under a certain condition, adopt the appropriate method, and shoot only under that condition, time permitting.

1. The Wind not only causes a bullet to drift to one side while shooting, but it reduces accuracy by increasing the sway of both the shooter's body and his pistol. The shooter should try to determine a proper compensating sight change if there is a constant side wind. If there is a head wind, take care that the wind is deflected away from the eyes by shooting glasses. Powder fragments and acrid fumes blown back into the face cause smarting and watering of the eyes. Body sway can be minimized by a concerted effort to resist the wind pressure. A slight increase in general muscular tension is necessary.

a. Wind shooting is conducive to jerking the trigger because as the arc of movement increases, the shooter develops a tendency to relax his positive trigger pressure. Usually the shooter is waiting for a more stable sight picture. His concentration on sight alignment will diminish and he will make an effort to set the shot off on the move as the sights pass the vicinity of the aiming point.

b. The obvious answer is to first wait for a lull in the wind; next, concentrate as one normally does on sight alignment. When the smallest arc of movement that is possible to obtain under existing conditions is achieved, positive pressure is applied to the trigger.

c. Do not continue the hold during extreme gusts. Always take advantage of a chance to rest. Each subsequent attempt to fire a shot should be made with a firm resolve to align the sights and to apply constantly increasing trigger pressure until the shot is fired.

d. The surprise shot continues to be the indicator, even under these conditions, of whether you are applying the fundamentals correctly. Your shot group will be somewhat larger as a result of the wind disturbance increasing the arc of movement, but the wild shots resulting from faulty sight alignment, flinching, jerking and over correction will be minimized.

e. Extensive practice under wind conditions is not recommended, but enough firing should be conducted under those conditions to familiarize the shooter with the technique and method best for him.

f. Changing of Wind: When shooting at 50 yards and the whole air mass is moving approximately the same velocity in one direction, fairly accurate sight corrections can be made for wind. When doing this, however, it is not wise to think an all-purpose correction has been made. The changing nature of the wind must be taken into account. The grass and weeds, etc., should be watched attentively while shooting to detect a change in the force and direction. A shot should be made only when wind conditions have been accurately determined.

g. Sometimes the necessity to shoot when the wind is gusty requires a shooter to shoot accurately in a very short time, say within two seconds. The successful firing of an accurate shot under such conditions will be achieved only if a shooter has remained in the firing position in the intervals between lulls. When shooting under such conditions, he should figure out the most advantageous posture for himself in which he can wait out the gusts of wind. As soon as there is a lull he will be able to take aim quickly and fire his shot.

h. To aid accurate shooting when a gusty wind is blowing and when the wind is changing, a shooter must alter his tempo of shooting. Sometimes he must shoot rapidly, sometimes shooting twice when the wind is quiet or when the lighting is right, sometimes taking fairly long breaks. Wait out the unfavorable conditions for making a shot; but watch your time!

i. In order to manage the difficulties arising during windy conditions a shooter should be prepared beforehand to change both the tempo of his shooting and alter his system of control as the situation in which he finds himself changes.

2. Adverse weather conditions such as cold, hot or rainy weather or extreme light conditions pose problems that can be solved in much the same manner as in wind shooting. Be determined to adhere to the fundamentals and ignore distractions to the competition. Compensate for disagreeable conditions.

a. It is advisable to carry a raincoat with you at all times and possibly a plastic cover for your gun box to keep your equipment dry. Most ranges, except for those at the National Matches, have covered firing points that help to keep the competitor dry during rainy weather. A rain suit or short heavy coat are the best garments for shooting in rain or cold windy weather. The folds and loose ends of a rain coat or overcoat flapping in the wind will cause body movement.

b. During cold weather the shooter must obviously wear warm clothing. Use insulated underwear to avoid wearing many layers of heavy clothing. When the shooter becomes shivering cold it is difficult to hold the sights in perfect alignment or retain sensitive trigger control. Hand warmers are very good and are small enough to keep in the gun box or pocket. Light weight lubricating oil must be used in cold weather to prevert malfunction of weapons.

c. During hot weather, perspiration becomes a problem. A sweat band on the forehead keeps the sweat out of the eyes and it is recommended that powdered rosin be used to dry the hand. When not on the firing line the shooter should relax in the shade. Covered firing points provide protection from the sun while shooting. Salt tablets prevent heat prostration. Eat lightly.

3. Changes in light intensity and direction have a great influence on the accuracy of aiming. Under changing conditions, the eye does not perceive the relationship of the front and rear sights consistently. There may be a change in the point of impact of the shot group on the target. Experienced shooters usually settle on one lighting condition when the cloud cover is changing, aiming only when the sun is shining brightly or shooting only when the targets are in the shade. The choice of a lighting condition must be made depending on the relative length of time that the targets are well lighted or shaded.

a. Light condition varies from extremely bright to very dim and the shooter must keep a record of the light conditions on every range he fires on in his scorebook. Some competitors are affected more by changes in light than others. A note should also be made as to how much his zero changes in these different light conditions. Sight should be blackened with care on bright days. As part of your shooting accessories, you should have both amber and green shooting glasses not only for light conditions but for protection against oil, powder fragments, fumes, wind and empty brass. Firing from an uncovered firing line usually requires different sight settings than the firing from under a shed. Ammunition should be kept out of the sun as its accuracy is affected if it is exposed to the direct rays of the sun.

b. A shooter must also be able to complete the match rapidly in order to avoid firing under marginal conditions. The necessity for rapid shooting arises when twilight sets in. There are times on any range when a shooter must either accept an interruption during a match or shoot at a stepped-up pace. For example, when the light on the target is shifting he must finish shooting before the sun's rays come through the target from the rear. This causes the target to appear blotched and makes accurate sighting and shooting difficult.

4. Our accomplishments on the firing line stem from out mental capacity to face up to the out of ordinary, and parlay these conditions into winning. Poor conditions must never become an excuse to quit or compromise. Good scores are produced by hard work in the application of the fundamentals regardless of the conditions. Proper control of the application of the fundamentals is the most important factor in shooting winning scores under adverse conditions.

F. TRAINING METHODS:

1. Competition: Any top shooter will agree with this word of advice: Shoot every match you can afford. The special conditions created by shoulder-to-shoulder competition can best be controlled by lessons learned in match experience. To learn how to apply this control to your slow fire technique is the result of continuous match competition.

If numerous matches are not available, try to make your practice sessions duplicate match conditions as nearly as possible.

2. Dry Firing: Developing the ability to apply the fundamentals to your shooting is a tedious, painstaking process. If all the effort is confined to range practice and competitive matches, years of hard work and great expense for ammunition are involved. The use of dry fire practice can reduce the cost in both respects.

Dry firing develops the ability to control your shooting in all the primary factors - coordination, eyesight, arc of movement, uniformity of applying fundamentals, analysis and correction, etc. Achieving the ability to control your body in its job of delivering a good shot is one of repetition of good shooting habits. Dry firing is a definite aid in this stage of development. To get the most out of your dry firing, use the appropriate work sheet to guide your work. Prepare and plan each shot as if it were a live round. Relax when you are ready and give yourself fire commands. Deliver the shot with the same amount of effort as in live practice. Use a target center on the bench to record your shot calls. If the shot calls embraced a detectable error, analyze and determine why the errors were in your performance. You may notice errors in your performance that have been hidden in the recoil and sound of the weapon as it is fired. Precise identification of these errors can be made only during dry fire sessions. A positive correction is necessary before proceeding to the next shot. A bulls-eye a blank wall or the open sky may be used to conduct dry firing.

Dry fire practice can be overdone. Initially, the new shooter should limit himself to ten minutes of effort. Later, as performance improves, maximum time should be about thirty minutes.

3. Ball and Dummy: Ball and dummy exercise is another important aid in accelerating your improvement. It is most effective when another person loads the weapon and observes the shooter as he attempts to fire. The coach loads either a live or dummy round at random. The shooter must never know whether he has a live or dummy round in the chamber. If the shooter is disturbing the weapon with muscle reactions in any way, the coach will be able to identify the error immediately. After identifying the error pattern, the coach and the shooter must agree on a positive correction. Ideally, the correction will prevent recurrence of the error. In most cases however, the coach and shooter must be satisfied with the error occuring less frequently.

4. Instruction in Fundamentals and Techniques Must not be Overlooked: Every shooter must be thoroughly schooled in pistol marksmanship fundamentals. His future success will be based on how well he masters the fundamentals and the techniques of employing them.

5. A Review of Fundamentals and Techniques must be conducted periodically. The shooter must be reminded of the fundamental points of pistol marksmanship to assure that his shooting skill will constantly improve. Each shooter must develop a personal technique of employing the fundamentals. Improvement is at a standstill when analysis of the technique no longer identifies and removes the flaws from poor performance.

CHAPTER VI

TECHNIQUE OF SUSTAINED FIRE

Timed and rapid fire stages can be stumbling blocks, especially if attempted in a haphazard manner. However, through the development of proper techniques and careful planning, you can improve your scores and become more consistent in your performance. A recent development in the thinking of shooters is the concept of a sustained fire technique instead of the more generally accepted idea of a separate method for each of the timed fire and rapid fire stages. Many shooters that have attained national and world recognition find a distinct problem in the build-up of tension caused by the time limitation of rapid fire. It has been found that the best method is to practice the technique developed for rapid fire by employing it during the timed fire phase as well. A further advantage is gained in that should an error pattern become apparent during timed fire, the shooter has ample opportunity to take corrective action. He can then test the effectiveness of the correction before being forced to employ it under the more strenuous conditions of the ten second time limitation of rapid fire.

A. EMPLOYMENT OF THE FUNDAMENTALS.

When a shooter makes his plan on the firing line to shoot timed and rapid fire, usually a number of things have already taken place. Normally, his slow fire has already been fired and the same fundamentals used there apply to the shooting of timed and rapid fire. The planning for a string of shots is an extension of the basic factors involved in firing slow fire shots with the addition of recovery and rhythm.

   1. Recovery is the return of the weapon to the original holding position in the center of the aiming area, accompanied by a natural alignment of the sights. If the shooter has a good solid stance, correct natual position, a firm grip, wrist stiff and elbow locked, the recovery is more natural and uniform. In the preliminary check out, if the weapon recovers to the right or to the left of the target center, it may be corrected by simply moving the rear foot in the direction of the error. If the sight alignment deviates, a compensating shift in grip must be made. Recovery must be accomplished as quickly as possible to allow more time for precise alignment of the sights and applying positive trigger pressure. The instant that the weapon was fired, the shooter must immediately resume the sequence of applying the fundamentals for the next shot. A distinct rhythm will develop that enables him to deliver his string on the target under control and within the time allowed.

Figure 6-1. The Stance, Position, and Grip Must Be Firm Enough to Absorb the Shock of the Recoil without the Wrist or Elbow Bending.

Figure 6-2. And Correct Enough So That Your Recovery Will Return the Weapon to Your Aiming Area Quickly and Precisely With a Center Hold and a Natural Alignment of Sights.

2. Developing a good rhythm is very difficult but is absolutely necessary for good, consistent time and rapid fire. By using a uniform technique, executing a planned sequence of actions correctly and applying careful timing for each shot, we achieve good rhythm. A regular cadence indicates smooth employment of the fundamentals provided the five-shot group is centered and tightly clustered. It is particularly true during rapid fire that you do not have time to correct minor errors in hold. Any attempt to correct minor errors in hold may result in loss of rhythm. This attempted correction causes a hesitation or pause in the sequence of firing a shot while the correction is being made and results in a speed-up of trigger pressure for the remaining shots of the string. The lack of rhythm causes more bad rapid fire strings than any other factor. The first shot must be fired within one second after the target turns in rapid fire. A common error is to try to attain a perfect sight picture in an effort to make the first shot an X thereby losing valuable time in getting the string started. When this happens, usually the shooter becomes worried about the time, loses his concentration, speeds up his deliver rate for the remaining shots of the string and as a result has poor rhythm and a bad string. Another common error is to shoot the first four rounds with good rhythm then knowing there is a lot of time left, hesitate and try to set up a perfect sight picture so as to shoot an X on the last shot. Usually this last shot will be bad because the shooter does not apply trigger pressure properly. He invariably becomes worried about the time, loses his concentration and forces the shot to fire. In doing so he disturbs the sight alignment by either jerking the trigger or heeling the shot. In timed and rapid fire, a rhythm or cadence of firing must be acquired. This rhythm is needed for coordination and also for assuring the shooter, in a subconscious manner, that an equal amount of time is being allotted for each shot, and that he is abreast of the time schedule. Any mechanical operation has a certain rhythm. Timed and rapid fire is definitely a mechanical operation.

B. TECHNIQUE OF SUSTAINED FIRE.

The shooter must employ a technique tailored to give him the ability to control the employment of the fundamentals under all conditions of competitive stress. The shooter must consider the following known factors which have a bearing on the control of a five-shot string of timed or rapid fire.

1. Find your aiming area on the edge of the target frame. Look directly at the faced target with your head in shooting position. Determine precisely where your aiming area is going to be when the target turns away. Relate this area to a spot on the edge of the frame that will be nearest you when the targets are edged. The time limitation precludes the luxury of looking at the target as it turns toward you so you can adjust your hold before applying positive trigger pressure for the first shot.

2. Stiffen your shooting arm as it extends the weapon toward the target and settles into the aiming area. Remember the degree of muscle tension required to give you solid arm control and a minimum arc of movement.

3. <u>You should look at the aiming area</u> and relate it to a spot on the edge of the target frame as you settle into a minimum arc of movement. Then shift the point of focus back to the rear sight before making a final point of focus on the front sight. This system is used to make absolutely sure the eyes are not focused somewhere between the front sight and the target.

4. <u>The shooter must never forget that once he attains final focus on the front sight he never again allows a focus shift until all five shots of the string have been fired.</u> To look at the target at any time during the string is inviting disaster. Trust your stance, position and grip to give your precise recovery and to maintain a minimum arc of movement within your aiming area.

5. <u>In rapid fire, the first shot should break soon after the target turns.</u> It is not necessary to try to get the first shot to break while the target is turning but it should break within one second. It is advisable to use the first motion of the target as the signal to apply positive, steadily increasing pressure on the trigger. The target's turning may sometimes produce a feeling of surprise and is accompanied by a momentary hesitation. This can cause a break in the shooter's composure and the firing of the first shot is delayed. By assuming a more determined attitude and stimulating your competitive aggressiveness you can overcome this problem. We suggest this approach: "When that target moves I am going to punch the 10 ring full of holes." You will be surprised at the effect this action has of eliminating any remaining doubts and at the resulting surge of confidence that it incurs.

6. <u>During recovery, reestablish sight alignment without a focus shift.</u> This action is important because a focus shift during recovery will delay the reestablishment of sight alignment. Approximately one-half second is needed between shots for this ill-advised operation and could total two full seconds of lost time. Successful rapid fire requires the use of ten full seconds for proper coordination and full control.

7. <u>If you allow your eyes to follow the pistol during recoil, you may inadvertently move your head out of its original position.</u> Any head movement during firing will disrupt the relationship between the aiming eye and the front and rear sight alignment. Correction will require a wrist movement which only artificially corrects the error. Upon recovery from recoil of the succeeding shot, the same error is once again apparent and likewise needs correction.

8. <u>Reaffirm your determination to concentrate upon sight alignment the instant positive trigger pressure is resumed.</u> Maintain your concentration on sight alignment until the pistol fires again.

9. <u>After the pistol fires it will be moved out of the normal hold area by the recoil of firing,</u> and it must be recovered instantly to the position it occupied prior to the dislocating effects of recoil. Recovery must be natural, uniform and quick.

10. <u>You must immediately reestablish a positive, steadily increasing pressure upon the trigger.</u> This should occur shortly before recovery is complete and the minimum arc of movement reestablished. The increasing pressure should neither be stopped nor varied in rate until the weapon has again been discharged. As soon as the positive, constantly increasing trigger pressure has been reapplied, shift your attention from thoughts of trigger control to the problem of sight alignment, just as you did on the first shot of the string.

11. <u>The sights will be in near perfect alignment at the end of recovery,</u> if the grip, control and head position are maintained. However, this ideal situation occurs only intermittently.

12. <u>Remind yourself that this technique, repeated for each shot, insures that continutiy is established from one shot to the next.</u> Assure yourself that you can deliver a successful string on the target with an absolute minimum of wasted thought and time by following this system.

C. COMMON DEFICIENCIES IN CONTROL: A number of deficiencies peculiar to timed and rapid fire are:

1. <u>Follow through,</u> applies to slow, timed and rapid fire and should not be confused with recovery. Follow through is the attempt by the shooter to keep everything exactly as it was set up until after the round is on its way to the target. Lack of follow through is a breakdown of one or more of the factors set up by the shooter to control a good shot. For example, lack of follow through might be caused by a speed up of trigger pressure resulting in anticipation of recoil and a heeled shot at one o'clock.

2. <u>Recovery</u> must be made quickly to allow time for aligning sights and positive trigger pressure. Recovering too slowly takes up excess time, alters the shooter's rhythm, and when he realizes that he has very little time left causes him to speed up his delivery rate. Each shot of a five shot string must be fired individually and uniformily, each one treated as a single shot. The shooter must see five distinct sight alignments.

3. <u>Grip:</u> An incorrect grip will cause misalignment of the sights on recovery after each round is fired. This is corrected by carefully shifting the grip before the next string. Any tilting or turning movement of the head from its normal level position will cause the weapon to appear to recover either to the right or left of the bull's eye. Both of these errors may cause a delay in firing on the shooter's part in an effort to correct them, or break his concentration on sight alignment, losing valuable time and causing a loss of rhythm. All these factors add up to a poor string of five shots. Check out and dryfire the position and grip during the three minute preparation period just prior to the range officer's command "LOAD."

4. <u>Calling The Shot Group:</u> Many shooters fail to remember each shot on the basis of five individual sight alignments and cannot call the shot group accurately. If the shot group call is made and the call and the group are not together, it is necessary to determine the case and apply positive correction. The weapon probably is not zeroed, the position was bad or the grip incorrect. If the shooter is sure of the zero of his weapon, then dry fire the position and grip before firing the next five shot string.

5. <u>Rhythm</u> is absolutely essential. A common error in sustained fire is trying to make the first shot an X and thereby losing valuable time in getting the string started. When this happens, the shooter usually has poor rhythm and a bad string. When a determined shooter causes the first shot to be fired on time, this same determination brings about a continuous application of the fundamentals that assures a rate of fire that will complete the string on time.

6. <u>In shooting rapid fire</u> the shooter does not have time to correct <u>minor errors</u> in hold. Trigger pressure is applied on the basis of sight alignment and <u>not</u> sight picture. The shooter should make every effort to keep his arc of movement at a minimum, continue positive trigger pressure, maintaining sight alignment, and shoot with a definite rhythm.

7. <u>Lack of A System:</u> When a shooter has a system to follow it relieves his mind so that he can concentrate on performance. Care should be taken during the early stages of instructional practice to comply with each of the items on the worksheets. As the shooter becomes more capable, only the key items of preparation, shot sequence, shot analysis and positive correction are relevant. Methodical repetition of these essential steps will instill in the shooter good shooting habits that will enable him to repeat a good shooting performance. Further, the rapid fire worksheet will help the shooter form the habit of not overlooking any factor that will help his shooting.

8. <u>Complete and instantaneous shot analysis</u> is a mandatory prerequisite for any improvement in your performance or scores. A mental impression of each sight alignment should come at the instant the shot breaks. Corrective measures to prevent the recurrence of a poor performance must be immediately applied. Much has been written about why we shoot poorly; however, be reminded that it is just as advantageous to <u>analyze why you are shooting well</u> on a particular day. It is more helpful to know the right way to perform than to have your mind cluttered with a multitude of "don'ts." Coaches in particular should concentrate on and emphasize the positive factors.

9. <u>Overeating</u> during the shooting day has lowered may aggregates. The delicate edge that a shooter attains before a match can be completely shattered by one hearty repast. The minimum arc of movement is greatly increased by the pulsations of a heartbeat imprisoned between an overloaded stomach and a suet incased ribcage.

10. <u>Inability to control mental processes</u> indicates a fear of failure or lack of motivation to do your best. The shooter must develop more effective method of stimulating confidence. Review the reasons why you are here as a shooter. You came to win the match. Encourage your competitive instincts by setting a goal as high as you can possibly reach.

11. **The shooter's concentration breaks as target turns.** More attention is required in developing a determined attitude and mental alertness. Review the system you use in starting positive trigger pressure and maintaining point of focus on front sight. Apply any correction needed. Remove all doubts as to the location of the center of the aiming area of the target in relation to the edge of the target frame during the preparation stage.

D. TRAINING METHODS.

1. **Frequent shoulder-to-shoulder competition** and regularly scheduled record practice on the firing range is the most effective method of accelerating your development as a top competitive shooter.

2. **To be most effective, each practice session must have a goal.** You should approach the training period with the idea that you are going to distinctly improve one aspect of your shooting technique and at the same time continue the general improvement of your ability to employ the fundamentals more effectively.

3. **To improve your ability to deliver your first shot quickly and accurately,** we advise a practice session of about ten rounds delivered in the following manner. Adjust the target turning mechanism to face the target and turn it away after one and one-half seconds. Use your normal preliminary preparation with maximum attention on delivering the first shot without hesitation as the target turns. Fire one shot only. Repeat the exercise ten times with sufficient time between shots to allow for mental reorganization and preparation. Fire two, fire-shot strings with the proper 10 second interval to establish your rhythm and then shoot a rapid fire, 20 shot match for record practice.

4. **To improve your ability to achieve rhythm and maintain a point focus on the front sight,** place a target on the frame backwards so that no bull's-eye or aiming point is visible. Assume your stance, position and grip with meticulous attention to detail. Without a point to aim at, you will find that you must trust your stance and position to maintain an acceptable arc of movement in the center of the aiming area on the blank target. You will find it easier to apply the fundamentals and discover that you can deliver the string with amazing accuracy. Rhythm and sight alignment can be maintained with a startling degree of control. This is because the distracting effects of having an exact point of aim has been eliminated. You have no way of knowing when a perfect hold occurs. A perfect sight picture is not necessary. You simply accept minor errors in hold caused by your minimum arc of movement and go ahead and follow your plan of delivery of each shot. After firing on the blank center you should immediately go into a rapid fire stage of fire with a normal target for record practice.

5. **Avoid training and shooting alone.** Use a training program that duplicates as near as possible the competitive atmosphere of a match. Develop and use a comprehensive plan that improves your ability to employ the fundamentals reliably under pressure and continuously strive for improvement.

6. **Dry firing practice** should be conducted with the same careful attention to detail as live ammunition practice. The shooter's rapid fire worksheet (para C, "Establish a System"), this Chapter, is a guide to perfecting your system of shooting control.

7. **Improvement of recovery** must be approached from two angles: Reestablish a hold in the center of the aiming area, and realignment of the front and rear sights in perfect relationship. Practice and repractice assuming a proper position that furnishes the shooter with a natural hold that points the shooting arm and weapon at the center of the aiming area. Get a proper grip and head position that gives the shooter a natural sight alignment. Quick recovery is essential. For example, with a 2 second interval to deliver a rapid fire shot, there should not be more than 1/2 to 1 full second devoted to recoil and recovery. At least 1 second of the interval must be used to dress up sight alignment while settling into a minimum arc of movement. The simultaneous application of positive trigger pressure may be delayed if either factor, hold or sight alignement, is imperfect.

E. WIND SHOOTING AND ADVERSE CONDITIONS: During timed and rapid fire, the shooter has to fire when the commands are given, wind or no wind. The means of overcoming this disturbing handicap are found in strenuous application of the fundamentals. Usually these efforts attain less positive results because the shooter cannot maintain his normal, minimum arc of movement in the wind. Concentration on sight alignment regardless of movement caused by wind will result in groups only slightly larger than those fired under ideal conditions.

1. During Wind Shooting: As the arc of movement increases during wind shooting, the shooter develops a tendency to relax his trigger pressure. He is waiting for a more stable sight picture. His concentration on sight alignment will diminish and he will make an effort to fire as the sights pass the vicinity of the target center. The obvious answer is to concentrate on sight alignment and maintain as small an arc of movement as possible and to start a constantly increasing pressure on the trigger until all shots are fired. Each attempt to fire a string of shots should be made with a firm resolve to align the sights for each shot and to apply increasing trigger pressure in spite of the increased arc of movement due to the wind. Your shot group will be larger, as a result of the increased arc of movement, but the wild shots resulting from faulty sight alignment, flinching, jerking and over-correction will be minimized.

a. Rhythm must be maintained, with the uncompromising determination not to hesitate in applying positive trigger pressure despite the abnormal movement of the shooting arm.

b. Extensive practice under windy conditions is not recommended but enough firing should be conducted under windy conditions to prevent a stampede to the nearest wind shelter when a wisp of air movement stirs the pine tops.

c. The shooter should not place too much reliance on indications of flags high above the line of targets and the firing line. In addition, do not accept the indications of flags flying at the edge of a forest, steep precipise, ravine, or depressions, since the wind speed, at various levels of the atmosphere and terrain are different. It is necessary to be guided by the indications of high grass, tall weeds, strips of paper, etc. in the vicinity, which are nearer the level of the weapon-target line.

d. It should also be kept in mind that wind can blow around terrain irregularities and create all kinds of turbulance. If flags were set up along the entire length of the range, they often would indicate a different, even opposite, wind direction. For this reason, the shooter should not always rely on one indication at the line of targets. Determine wind direction and intensity for the entire length of the range, by carefully observing the motion of grass and bushes located between the firing line and the target.

e. With time, the shooter will develop a subconscious feeling and acquire experience that enables him to become rapidly oriented to wind conditions and to make the necessary corrections for carrying out accurate fire under adverse conditions.

2. Adverse weather conditions such as cold, hot or rainy weather or extreme light conditions pose problems that can be solved in the same manner as in wind shooting. Be determined to adhere the fundamentals and ignore the distraction of adverse weather.

a. It is advisable to carry a raincoat with you at all times and a plastic cover for your gun box to keep your equipment dry. Most ranges have covered firing points that help to keep the competitors dry during rainy weather.

b. During cold weather the shooter must obviously wear warm clothing to include insulated underwear. When the shooter becomes shivering cold it is difficult to hold the sights in perfect alignment, or retain sensitive trigger control. Hand warmers are very good and are small enough to keep in the gun box or pocket. Light weight lubricating oil must be used in cold weather to prevent malfunction of weapons.

c. During hot weather prespiration becomes a problem. A sweat band on the forehead keeps sweat out of the eyes and it is recommended that powdered rosin be used to dry the hands. When not on the firing line the shooter should relax in the shade. Here again covered firing points provide protection from the sun while shooting. Salt tablets prevent heat prostration. Eat lightly.

d. Effect of temperature on the shot dispersion:

(1) The lower the air temperature, the greater the air density. A bullet travelling in denser air encounters a larger number of air particles, with the result that it loses its initial velocity rapidly. Therefore, when shooting in cold weather, the bullet velocity decreases somewhat and the center of impact moves downward slightly.

(2) In firing a large number of rounds for an extensive period of time, when the pistol barrel becomes hot, the shooter should not permit a round to remain in the chamber too long. The relatively high temperature of the barrel is transferred to the propellant by means of the cartridge case, and can lead to a change in center of impact and to high shots, depending upon the length of time the round remains in the hot chamber.

3. <u>Light varies from extremely bright to very dim</u> and the shooter must keep a record of light conditions on every range fired on in his score book. Some competitors are affected more by changes in light than others. A note should be made as to how much his zero changes in the different light conditions. Sights should be blackened with care on bright days. As a part of the shooting accessories, you should have both amber and green shooting glasses not only for light conditions but for protection against oil, wind and empty brass. Firing from an uncovered firing line usually requires different sight settings than the firing from under a shed. Ammunition should be kept out of the sun as its accuracy is affected if it is exposed to the direct rays of the sun.

4. <u>The major portion of our accomplishments on the firing line stems from our mental capacity</u> to face up to the out of the ordinary and parlay these conditions into a winning margin. Poor conditions must never become an excuse for expending less effort and consequently a poor performance. Good scores are produced by hard work in the application of the fundamentals regardless of the conditions. Proper application of the fundamentals is the most important factor in shooting winning scores under adverse conditions.

CHAPTER VII

MENTAL DISCIPLINE

A. PURPOSE: The purpose of this chapter is to acquaint you with the need for and the method of controlling your mental and emotional processes and extending your span of mental concentration while under conditions of competitive stress.

B. GENERAL: Mental discipline is the broad term used in describing the shooter's actions and reactions when facing competitive pressure. A distinguishing feature of successful competitive shooting is that it is associated with overcoming obstacles and difficulties which require the utmost exertion of a person's mental capacity. The ability to keep control of oneself, to force oneself to overcome difficulties, and to maintain presence of mind in any difficult situation is a necessary human quality. With out this quality, you will not shoot high scores in a match. To sustain mental discipline, you must have high moral qualities, a sense of duty and responsibility to the team and a sense of honor. These traits are the source of the will to win. In moments of crisis, they help you to mobilize all your resources for victory. No person is born with these qualities. They are partly developed in the course of the shooter's life and the activities of daily living. Good marksmanship training will solidify these traits and develop the minds ability to control mental processes.

C. ESSENTIAL TO MARKSMANSHIP

1. Mental control is essential to marksmanship. Mastery of the physical skills alone does not provide the control of performance necessary to compete at the highest level. Emphasis must be placed on how and what to think. The capacity for intense concentration will provide for exacting control. Coordination of the essential factors is necessary for the delivery of an accurate shot on the target.

2. Mental discipline provides the control you must have of your mental faculties to maintain confidence, positive thinking, and sustain the ability to duplicate a successful performance. Mental discipline will help to avoid overconfidence, pessimism and withstand conditions that disrupt mental tranquility. It also provides the emotional stability necessary for the development of a champion shooter and confidence in his ability to successfully employ the basic skills of marksmanship for a dependable performance under all types of stress.

D. DEVELOPING MENTAL DISCIPLINE AND CONFIDENCE: The continuously repeated, successful execution of a completely planned shot results in the gradual development of mental discipline. If your mental discipline has developed sufficient force you will be able to control your thoughts and exercise unhampered mental concentration. Also, your preparations and shooting routines will always be the same.

1. Response to a problem: Psychologists have determined that there are four basic methods of responding to a problem. Two methods are positive and classified as direct or indirect. Two methods are negative, classified as retreat and evasion.

a. Positive Response.

(1) The direct, positive approach. This is the self-confident, self-sufficeint, direct, positive attack. You realistically face the facts, analyze them, identify and evaluate the obstacles to a successful solution. You know what you want to accomplish and you take direct steps to attain it.

(2) The indirect, substitute or compromise approach. This is characterized by small, diffident, tentative, indirect action. Sidestepping leads to seeking short-cuts. When the probable solution is tried, there is much fervent hoping that the fates are on your side. You are only hinting and probing instead of establishing definitely what you need to do. There is only a minimum of positive effort here.

b. Negative response.

(1) The negative retreat: The failure to give the honest try to see what you are capable of accomplishing. Surrendering without a sincere effort. The flight habit can become chronic. This is the man that cannot accept the responsibility for a mistake or failure. A bad shot produces excuses.

(2) Evading the issue: Evasion is the lack of incentive. Why? is the approach. Why do I have to do better than anyone else? If the desire to excel is not there, you will never aimlessly or otherwise achieve the degree of accomplishment that crowns the champion.

2. Analyze the problem.

a. Psychologists have discovered that one of the chief reasons for difficulty in the solution of problems is inability to soundly analyze. Pose a clearcut plan of action in full array. Face the specific difficulty and make a determined effort to break it down. If it can be identified, there is a solution for it. There are shooters on your team or some other team that are operating without this specific problem putting a brake on their performance. Talk it out. A communal pondering session will break it wide open.

b. There is a four-point system of analyzing and solving specific problems. It reduces the whole big problem to four small ones: "STEPS IN THE PLANNING"; " SPECIFIC DIFFICULTIES"; "SUCCESSFUL SOLUTIONS"; "DOUBTFUL OR NO WORKABLE SOLUTION. " Weigh your "specific difficulties" and "doubtful solutions" and start an improvement campaign to resolve each area of difficiency

3. Confidence. Confidence results from repeatedly bringing under control all the factors that create conditions for firing an accurate shot. An accurate shot is one that hits the center of the target. You must have confidence to shoot well. Confidence in what? How do you get it? How do we keep it once it is obtained?

a. You must have confidence in the fundamentals. You must be convinced that if you control their employment correctly, you will achieve excellent results.

b. You must also have confidence in your ability to execute the proven fundamentals correctly. You will have proven your ability to do this in your practice sessions.

c. Think big! Think positive! "I will do it, " and you will succeed. However, as soon as you admit the slightest possibility of failure, your chance of success is questionable.

d. It has been said that a shooter must have an open mind, implying that we must have the ability to accept new ideas. What we should also strive for is a mind that is open to positive thoughts and completely closed to negative thoughts. You have heard so many times "Don't jerk that trigger. " True as this axiom may be, it is of no advantage to have this thought enter your mind when you are trying to get off a shot. It is negative, it implies failure. Such thinking continually occupies your mind with something you don't want to do, rather than something you should do. Would it not be more advantageous to think, "I must follow through, for when I do this, I will get an "X". This is the positive side of the picture, it implies success. It gives you something that you should do rather than something you should not do. What the shooter needs is a mind full of positive "do's and "wills." There is no room or necessity for those distracting "don'ts" and can'ts. " However, just thinking positively is not enough; we still must have definite ideas of how we are going to employ positive thoughts. There is no room for vagueness or vacillation in our technique of shooting.

e. A confident attitude adversely affects your competitirs. A match is generally conceded to a small number of confident individuals who expect to win. Confidence is contagious and favorably affects your teammates. Smile. Give no comfort to your competition by revealing by word or by act that anything is wrong that might affect your chances of winning the match.

4. Channeled mental effort resists the tendency of the mind to drift during the period when intense concentration on the relationship of the front and rear sights is essential.

a. Channel mental effort relentlessly toward the final act.

b. Complete exclusion of extraneous thoughts for a brief period (three to six seconds) is necessary for controlled delivery of the shot.

c. Prior planning of the sequence of action gradually enables the shooters to sustain concentration for a longer period.

d. Coordination of thought and action is the result of experience obtained through extensive practice and match shooting where the same satisfactory plan of action is followed repeatedly. Precise coordination is absolutely necessary in controlling the delivery of each shot during the entire match. Split second coordination and timing are maintained by frequent practice. When the practice time is insufficient, do not be overconfident and expect to be able to sustain coordination through prolonged match shooting conditions.

E. WHY CAN'T YOU BE A WINNER? (THE DANGER OF NEGATIVE THINKING.)

1. Who won the last match in which you participated? If you did not win, what was the reason?

Why is it so difficult to shoot championship scores? It is not that most of us have not been taught the fundamentals of shooting, the fault usually lies in that we open our minds up to thousands of negative reasons why we cannot shoot good scores.

The following is a discussion of each of the reasons that bring about a poor performance, and what can be done about them:

a. When the weather is bad, it is simple to say "It is raining, snowing, the wind is blowing. All my scores are going to be bad." This may be a true assumption. You can follow this vein of thought throughout the match and you probably will continue to shoot just average scores as compared to your competitors.

Why not think and convince your self that good winning scores have and will be fired under the same bad conditions. Positive application of the fundamentals has produced good results in spite of the numerous difficulties. If your thoughts are directed strongly enough towards planning and executing a controlled performance, you will not have time to worry about the weather.

b. Don't "Sunday - morning - quarter back" the operation of the range. Convince yourself that, "As long as there is a target to shoot at and I have the proper amount of time to shoot, I will shoot good scores."

c. Have you asked yourself, "why must I shoot exceptional scores?" The answer to this question will vary with each shooter. You must be motivated to constantly improve your performance. One of the most common excuses for not trying your best is because there is no challenging competition. A tendency to accept a passable score in a match becomes a habit. You tolerate an average performance without becoming alarmed. Regardless of the competitive ability present, you must employ the fundamentals to the utmost of your ability. You must retain not only the desire to win, but strive to set new records at all times. Failure to accept the challenge will cause a decline into the habit of treating your shooting as a daily task instead of a challenging adventure.

d. The main components necessary to shoot championship scores are an accurate gun, good ammunition, an individual with the ability (physical and mental) and the desire to be a champion. Therefore every time you let the thought of inferior equipment enter your mind, STOP! Think: "This gun and ammunition will shoot possibles if I control it."

e. The potential winner is always thinking about applying his plan of action and not about how he is going to beat you. He knows that most of the other competitors are beating themselves with their own uncontrolled thoughts. You can be one step ahead of all your competitors by directing your mental effort toward your plan of controlling each shot.

f. There is a first time for winning in shooting as in everything else. A first time for a national champion to be beaten, and a first time for you to become a national champion. If you want to win all the marbles, you can. The best way is to believe you are as qualified to win as anyone else. Make up your mind that you are going to shoot your next tournament as one big match. Let the individual stages and gun aggregates take care of themselves. A good performance on each individual shot is now your aim.

g. Carelessness is a state of mind that overwhelms an individual who is aimless and haphazard in his approach to a challenging task. Organization of all the factors having a bearing on the task will in most instances assure that the action will be successfully executed.

h. Overconfidence dulls your normal responses. You ignore or are unconscious of the development of unfavorable conditions. False assurance can upset the sensitive balance on which your performance depends. Do not relax your determination to work hard even if competition is not keen. Strive to reach a happy medium between overconfidence and pessimism.

i. Pessimism detracts from your ability to concentrate. Anxiety over possible failure undermines the ability to control the shot. Impatience and uncontrolled actions are the results. A negative approach hampers the repetition of a uniform, satisfactory performance.

j. Avoid distracting conditions which you know will upset you. Avoid emotional upset such as anger, worry, giving up under adverse conditions or after unsatisfactory shots. Ignore boasts, rumors, misinformation, and snide remarks. Avoid adding up individual shots as the buildup to the final scores.

F. MATCH PRESSURE: If you think that you and you alone have the problem of match pressure, look around - we all have it. The man who has never experienced match pressure has never been in a position to win a match. What is the difference? What is the dividing line between champion and plinker? Both may shoot comparable scores in practice, yet one is invariably at the top of the list and the other at the bottom. The dividing line is clear and obvious; the ability or lack of ability to control their thinking. Mental discipline. Some have learned to control their emotions and anxieties and go right ahead and perform within their capabilities. Others, even with years of experience pressure themselves out of the competition every time they step up to the firing line.

1. First, in the treatment of match pressure, we must find what causes it. Without knowing the reasons, we can never combat it. Match pressure is simply a condition created by suspense, and the uncertainty and anxiety which generally accompanies suspense. For example, it is easy for the relatively inexperienced competitor to feel suspense building up as he finds himself amassing a superior score; or for even the experienced competitor to feel, as he nears the finish of a match, knowing he can win. This is when worry and fear creeps in and, unless controlled, the resultant tension will undermine efforts for maximum performance.

2. The main thing that will help a shooter under these conditions is experience. Long hours of practice in working on his shortcomings and tournament participation against the best competition will serve to gradually calm our emotions and anxieties when under stress. The champions, in spite of their nervousness in match competition, mobilize all their energies and resources and on occasion, do even better in a match than in practice.

The emotional and physical upsets of competitive stress are experienced differently by different persons. The condition varies for every shooter both in its character and in its intensity. However, regardless of experience or ability to exercise self-discipline, shooters are to some degree nervous in competition. The better you are trained, the more confidence you will have. If you have trained under conditions approximating match conditions and have participated in many tournaments in the past, you will be less nervous. At the beginning of a shooting season, even with experience, you may be somewhat nervous. It is important that you must not remain passive to these disturbances. Do not let yourself become a victim of your emotions. Resist stubbornly and force yourself to shoot to win. If you feel that nervousness in competition is unknown to you, you may be indifferent to the best interests of the group. You may lack an elementary understanding of pride in doing a job well. You are showing indifference to one of the strongest, natural excitements which present a challenge to the human animal. When anxious, you add to your distress when you feel that everyone is watching you. Yet with all this, our counterpart, the Champion, appears to be calm and enjoying himself. Let's face it, he is!

3. How do you control match pressure? First, realize that it can be controlled and actually used to your advantage. Individuals have learned to control their shooting to the extent that their match and practice scores don't vary appreciably.

a. Prior mental determination. This is the most helpful factor that is available to you. By thinking through the correct procedure for firing each shot, just before you shoot, you can virtually eliminate distraction. If you fail to do this and approach the shot without a preconceived plan of attack, your results at best will be erratic.

b. Channel your thinking to the more important fundamentals. You must continually think fundamentals and review them in your mind. Train yourself so that as many of these fundamentals as possible are executed automatically without tedious effort on your part. When you do this, you have only the most difficult fundamentals to contend with in the actual firing. This will enable you to direct all of your mental and physical efforts toward keeping your eyes focused on the front sight and following through.

c. Establish a Routine: Keep from becoming excited. In establishing a routine, you eliminate the possibility of forgetting some trivial item of preparation or technique that may throw you off balance.

d. Work on each shot individually. Each shot must be treated as an individual task. There is no reason to believe that because your first shot was bad, your next one will be the same. Nor is it logical that if your first three shots were good, you have a guarantee that those to follow will also be good. Each one is merely a representation of your ability to apply the fundamentals. Your performance will vary if you let it.

e. Relax your mind. Right from the time you get up in the morning. Nothing will put you in a greater state of mental agitation than to have to rush through breakfast and rush to make your relay. If this happens, your score is ruined at about the third red light you hit. Take it easy. Shooting is fun, enjoy it.

f. Practice Tranquility. Are you the guy that loses his temper every time he has a bad shot? With whom are you mad? You are doing nothing more than admonishing yourself for your vacillation in the execution of a shot. If you had worked a little harder on applying the control factors, the shot would have been better. On the other hand if you do everything within your power to make the shot good and for some reason or other it is not good, you should have no cause for undue irritation. Although you must exert all of your mental and physical ability toward shooting a good score, infrequently you will fail to do this. Needless to say that when this happens, if you chastise yourself severely, or fall into a fit of depression because of poor score, you will hurt your performance for the rest of the match. It is not intended that you laugh off or treat lightly a poor performance; however, you must possess the presence of mind to accept the bitter with the sweet. Preparing, planning, relaxing and care in delivering the shot with careful analysis and positive corrective measures, is the cycle of action you must force yourself to conform to. You can then be assured that the next shot will be delivered under the most precise control you are capable of exerting.

g. Match Experience. Without question, competitive experience is one of the ingredients necessary to an accomplished competitor. However, experience alone is of limited value. You must flavor experience with an accurate and honest evaluation of performance. You must strive for increasing mental control. It is often left out of training until the physical ability to shoot far exceeds the ability to exercise mental control.

h. Argue with your Subconscious. Not only argue with it but win the argument. Even as you are reading this you are hearing that little voice in the back of your mind that keeps saying "Yes, this sort of thing may work for Joe, but I know damn well I am going to goof the next time I get close to a winning score." Whose voice is this? Where did all these ideas come from in the first place? Where did this little guy get all his knowledge? Let us be realistic. Your conscious mind puts these ideas into your subconscious, so don't ever believe that you can not over power it. It is not easy. He has been saying what he pleased for years and now he isn't to be routed easily. But don't give in to him and eventually you will find that the subconscious mind is not in conflict with your conscious efforts.

k. With all of this emphasis on the positive approach you are now going to get two big "don'ts."

(1) Don't expect spectacular results the first time you try mental discipline. There is coordination of employment of the fundamentals to be mastered. If you find that you exercise satisfactory control only for a short period of time, work on extending this period by practicing and perfecting your system. Remember that your returns are in proportion to your investment.

(2) Don't use alcohol and drugs. One or both of these may control some of the symtoms brought about by match pressure. However, in doing so they incapacitate you in other ways that will prevent good performance.

G. REDUCING TENSION AND ATTAINING RELAXATION

1. **Types of Tension:**

a. Normal tension is the prevailing condition of any organism when it is mustering its strength to cope with a difficult situation. All animals, including man, tense in situations which involve the security of themselves and their loved ones.

b. Pathological tension is an exaggeration of normal tension and fairly rare. This type of tension usually requires that the subject be put under the care of a physician.

c. The vast majority of people and shooters who are concerned with tension have nothing more than normal tension. All they need is a technique for relaxing. You should know what tension is and a few hints on how to minimize its effects.

2. **In normal tension**, your body undergoes certain definite changes. Adrenalin pours into your bloodstream and your liver releases sugar, giving a supply of energy to your muscles. Your entire nervous system shifts into high gear. It causes your sense of smell, hearing and sight to become sharpened and all your mental faculties to become razor keen. Your stepped-up nervous system also causes the large voluntary muscles of your legs, arms and torso to contract, ready for action. The muscles of your digestive tract cause your digestion to slow down for a while. Your chest and arteria muscles contract slightly so that your breathing becomes a bit shallower and your blood pressure increases. When all these things are happening, you are experiencing normal tension. Most of us experience this kind of tension one or more times a day. When the problem which caused you to be tense has been solved, your tension will subside and you will return to a normal state of relaxation. It may leave slowly but it will leave. Normal tension is self-limiting, it does not continue unabated after you need it.

3. **Pathological tension** is when your whole body over-reacts, as if the difficulty confronting it were a life or death matter. It is the kind of reaction a normal person would have only in an extremely dangerous situation. In pathological tension, blood pressure, heartbeat and pulse go way up and stay up. Excessive adrenalin may result in jitteriness, flushing and trembling. The digestive actions of the stomach usually stop entirely and will not resume, causing loss of appetite or indigestion. Muscles tense for action but may end by cramping. There is rapid, shallow breathing to the point of dizziness. The inevitable, and often swift result is a sense of deadening fatigue. Normal tension may make you feel exhausted too, but not to this degree.

4. **Tension Reducing Techniques:**

Take a breather. Breathe deeply, three times, very slowly; at the end of each exhalation, hold your breath as long as possible. When you have finished, you should feel noticeable relaxed and much-calmer. By forcing yourself to breathe deeply, you break the tension of your voluntary breathing muscles. This causes the involuntary muscles of the lungs, gastro-intestinal tract and heart to relax too. This is the simplest method for relaxing. For some, it can be used to end tension completely. It can be used by others for temporary relief when they do not wish to "let down" completely.

b. Let go. Sit down and let your head droop forward. Try to actually concentrate on relaxing the muscles. Make one arm relax completely; then the other. Now let your legs go completely limp; now your torso muscles. Stay in this posture for several minutes. Momentarily divorce the competition completely from your mind. This technique is aimed at relaxing the voluntary muscles. It is especially effective when you have had to maintain normal tension for several hours on end.

c. Stop and Think. When the tension-making job allows a respite, sit down and calmly review the things in your life that you value highly. Think of the long range purpose of your life, of the people you love, the things you really want. In a few minutes you may notice that you have involuntarily taken a deep breath. This is a sign that tension is dropping away rapidly. When you tense to face a difficult situation, you tend to exaggerate its importance. Judgment and reason can quickly change this mental state when it is time to relax again.

d. Take a Break. This is a "Remote Control" technique for dealing with normal tension. Simply take a break for ten full minutes every hour. You may find that this allows you to ease out of your working tension more quickly and easily.

e. Shift Into Low. Taper off at the end of the day by becoming involved in a diverting activity. If you like handiwork, pick a kind which is interesting but not too creative. Soap sculpture, finger painting, woodworking, and gardening all are excellent low-gear activities that will help you to "simmer down." This kind of tension-remover is aimed at changing your mental "set." It is helpful for those who have to operate at top capacity. After stimulation, a part of your mental capacity will continue to be aroused. To slow you down when you are in this state of mind, you require something which is engrossing but which demands nothing of you intellectually. Television entertainment and simple handicrafts are ideal.

f. These techniques are based on the fact that tension can be ended in two distinct ways: through the relaxation of your voluntary and involuntary muscles; and by changing your mental "set." If you achieve either, you modify the other and hasten the process of normal relaxation.

H. YOU CAN WIN!

1. Confidence furnishes the alloy to stiffen the will to win and not give up or compromise. Confidence is based on a full grasp of the complete technique of controlling employment of the fundamentals. Confidence combined with knowledge, good physical condition and a determination to win, will allow you to perform at your best. A chance at greatness lies in each man's grasp. You must have confidence that you are capable of a performance exceeding any previous level of personal accomplishment. Know that you can win if that is what you set out to do.

2. Be a hungary shooter. The slashing onslaught of a voracious appetite for victory destroys the resolve of the lesser competitor.

SECTION THREE

COMPETITIVE PHYSICAL FITNESS

CHAPTER VIII

PHYSICAL CONDITIONING

A. GENERAL

1. The objective of physical training in a pistol marksmanship training program is to condition the shooter physically, to better withstand the rigors of match conditions. An individual in good physical condition has better developed reactions, better control of his muscles and better endurance; all of which promote consistency in performance.

2. It is important that physical training not be of haphazard nature, nor should it be timed immediately before a pistol match. A shooter should perform physical exercises regularly, both during the preparation period between shooting seasons and during the period when the shooter is training for tournament participation. Morning limbering up exercises are important in this connection, and they should become a part of a shooter's daily routine. It has been found that a physical training program should be discontinued approximately 3 days prior to a match and resumed immediately thereafter.

3. Physical Conditioning must consist of exercises of a general nature directed toward strengthening the muscles, proper breathing, developing body flexibility and precision of movement. The requirements of marksmanship are such that drills must consist of exercises which develop the muscles and flexors of the arms and fingers, and the muscles of the shoulders and waist. A certain amount of static tension (dynamic) type exercise is valuable if it is not overdone.

4. Whenever the shooter exercises, he must put the maximum effort into the exercise. Merely going through the motions of an exercise is of no advantage. Physical conditioning is a gradual process and results will not be apparent immediately. As the shooter's physical condition improves, the number of repetitions may be gradually increased. Heavy exercise such as serious weight lifting should be discouraged.

5. Any sport that encourages regular physical activity is beneficial to a shooter. It is recommended that each shooter cultivate an interest in a sport that will insure sufficient exercises for all around physical fitness.

6. A muscle builds more rapidly under tension applied vigorously.

7. The stronger the muscle structure is developed, the surer movement can be coordinated and positions held. Besides general conditioning practices, durable muscle tension exercises of the trunk, shoulder and arm muscles make the most sense. Resistance exercises and grip exercises are in order. Physical training should take place at least three times a week for 30 minutes to an hour.

8. Sleep: During the training period the shooter needs plenty of sleep to give all the organs a chance for sufficient rest. Eight hours should be the rest interval. Before matches, insomnia sometimes occurs due to excitement. Under such conditions no sleeping pills should be taken the night before a match for they work out unfavorably the next day. Short walks in the evening, warm showers or a small snack will sometimes induce sleep.

9. Detrimental habits: Nicotine, caffeine and alcohol reduce the performance ability of the body and effect the ability to concentrate. (See Chapter X, "Effects of Alcohol, Coffee, Tabacco and Drugs.").

10. Overall behavior: Before a match the shooter should avoid all types of excitement. For example, he should not drive fast and, if possible, arrive at the range one-half hour before the beginning of the match. That will give him plenty of time for his last preparations and he can prepare himself inwardly for the test ahead. The individual feeling of well being is the best measure of whether or not your living habits and daily routine is in the best interest of your shooting.

B. BASIS FOR A GOOD PHYSICAL CONDITION.

A physical training program should be progressive. It is not necessary or is it generally considered wise to strive for the peak condition sought by a track athlete or a professional football player. Violent and strenuous athletics which may result in injuries should be avoided.

The competition shooter must possess the following basic physical and psycho-physiological characteristics:

1. An adequately developed muscular system (this is especially true for the muscles of the abdomen, arms, and legs) and the endurance to fire many shots without preceptible worsening of results.

2. Lungs must have a high oxygen assimilation factor so that long pauses between inhalations will not cause oxygen starvation.

NOTE: A smoker's lungs do not have a desirable oxygen assimilation factor.

3. Precision and coordination of bodily actions and thoughts. The physical training of a pistol shooter must be directed to the development of these qualities.

C. TYPE OF EXERCISE.

There are many different general types of exercises and activities that a shooter can use to his advantage.

1. Walking is a very good exercise. When walking, don't just take a slow window shopping walk. To get any good out of it, you must make the walk very brisk.

2. Running: Results already obtained indicate a running program improves overall physical fitness, especially in endurance capacity and overall improvement of the heart, lungs, and the entire circulatory system.

Running and walking for a period of 12 minutes at least three times a week is, in itself, a splendid conditioner. Here again, the individual must apply himself diligently for the duration of the exercise period.

3. A series of mild, non-strenuous exercises of the type that require body bending, stretching, deep breathing and moderate muscular tension are best suited to obtaining a condition defined as good body tone and a feeling of well-being. Sore, aching muscles tend to fatigue quickly, and nervous tremor usually results.

4. In Swimming almost all of the muscles get a workout. Here again, the exercise should be pursued with moderation.

5. A good exercise to build the wrist and arm muscles in the wrist and forearm developer, roll-up exercise. A mop handle, a short length of rope and a weight. Roll it up and let it down slowly.

6. A method of developing the grip is by using a sponge rubber ball about 3" in diameter, cut in half. Squeeze the ball with the shooting hand. You can take this aid with you almost any place you go, and exercise any time that you are not using your shooting hand.

D. THE PISTOL TEAM DAILY DOZEN EXERCISES.

The Pistol Team Daily Dozen was especially developed to affect those muscles used in pistol shooting. Figures 8-1 thru 8-12 will assist the instructor in understanding how these exercises are accomplished.

1. Warm-Up: A four count exercise done in moderate cadence. This exercise is designed to get you ready for the forthcoming exercises. Starting position is standing with feet spread approximately 12 inches apart, hands extended overhead. At the count of one, bend at the waist and knees,

reach down between the legs, and place hands on ground. On the count of two, straighten body up, extending the hands over the head; at the count of three, perform same as number one; at the count of four, repeat number two.

2. Cat Stretch: The starting position is a modified leaning rest, the buttocks being higher. This is a four count exercise. Count of 1 is upward, pushing the buttocks higher. Count of 2, back to starting position. The count of 3 upward and on the count of 4, back to the starting position. This exercise uses the back and shoulder muscles.

3. Body Twister: The starting position is standing with arms extended paralled with ground, feet spread approximately twelve inches apart. This is a four count exercise. At the count of one, swing the arms to the right, keep the shoulders and arms rigid so the twisting movement is from the waist. On the count of two, swing to the right and front. At count of three, repeat count one to the left. At count of four, face to front. This uses the muscles along the sides and back of the trunk of the body.

4. Push-Up: The starting position is standing. This is a four count exercise. At the count of one, squat with hands on ground; count two, extend legs. Count three, cause the body to move downward; keep the body straight at all times. At the count of four recover to the raised position. Continue counts three and four as desired. End exercise by recovering to standing position. This uses the arms and shoulder muscles.

5. Back Bender: The starting position is standing with the feet spread twelve inches apart, hands on back of neck. On the count of one, bend back at the waist. On the count of two, recover. Count of three, bend backward at the waist; count of four, recover. This uses the back and stomach muscles.

6. Hip and Leg Spreader: The starting position is with the hands and toes on the ground. This is a four count exercise. At the count of one bend the elbows and touch the chin to the ground at the same time extending the left leg back and up. Count two, recover. The counts of three and four are repetitions using the right leg. This uses the arm and leg muscles.

7. Shoulder Exerciser: Starting position is standing with the feet spread and hands and arms at the sides. This is a four count exercise. At the count of one, extend the arms sideward, parallel to the ground. Count of two, rotate arms. Count of three, touch shoulder with hands. Count of four, recover. This exercise is to be done with dumbbells if available. This uses the muscles of the arm and the shoulder muscles.

8. Abdominal Kick: The starting position is lying flat with the arms extended to the side; at the count of one, raise your body with the weight on the buttocks and hands, legs straight together, about 15 degrees off the ground. At the count of two raise the legs toward the chest. Count of three, extend the legs outward, keeping the feet off the ground. Count of four, recover to starting position. This uses the stomach and leg muscles.

9. Side Bender: The starting position is standing with the feet together, arms at sides. At count of one, extend arms overhead, shift weight to bended left leg. On the count of two, bend at the waist to the side, count of three, recover to count one. Count of four, recover to starting position. Count 5, 6, 7, and 8 are a repetition, only bend to right. This uses the muscles along the sides of the body.

10. Body Kick: The starting position is flat on the back, arms behind head. At the count of one raise the body at the waist. Count two, resume flat position. At the count of three raise body and lift the right leg upward. Count of four, drop the right leg and lift the left leg. Count of five, drop left leg and lift right leg. Count of six, resume flat position. This uses the stomach and leg muscles.

11. Tricep Exerciser: The starting position is standing, arms at sides. At count of one, bend forward at the waist, arms hanging down. Count of two, raise arms parallel with the body. At the count of three, extend the arms to the left foot. Count of four, recover to count two. Count of five, extend the arms to the right foot. Count of six, recover to starting position This exercise is to be done with dumbbells if available. This uses the tricep muscles.

12. _Leg Spreader:_ The starting position is lying flat for count one. At the count of two, throw the legs back over the head, legs spread; extend the arms parallel with the ground. At the count of three, recover and reach for ankles. At count of four, resume lying flat. Count of five, spread legs and arms. Count of six, recover to count one. This uses the leg and stomach muscles.

To be effective, physical training for the pistol shooter must be realistic and continuous. The objective is to continue to condition the body so that the general health is excellent and that the muscular and nervous systems are fully capable of withstanding the grind of match conditions and enable the shooter to continue to assert his utmost skill.

Figure 8-1

Figure 8-2

Figure 8-3

PUSH UP IV

Figure 8-4

BACK BENDER V

Figure 8-5

HIP & LEG SPREADER VI

Figure 8-6

SHOULDER BUILDER VII

Figure 8-7

67

Figure 8-8

Figure 8-9

Figure 8-10

TRICEP
BUILDER
XI

START   1   2-4   3   5   6

Figure 8-11

LEG SPREADER
XII

START — I   2   3

4   5   6

Figure 8-12

CHAPTER IX

DIET AND HEALTH OF THE COMPETITIVE PISTOL SHOOTER

A. GENERAL.

What is meant by good nutrition? Gayelord Hauser, America's famed Diet and Health specialist, answers as follows: "First, it is adequate nutrition, giving the individual cells of the body not only the quantity but also the quality of nourishment they require. Second, balanced nutrition, supplying the body cells with vital nutrients in the proper proportion. As a simplified illustration, think of your body as a motor car. It is made of protein, inside and out. Arteries, glands, colon, connective tissue; muscles, skin, bones, hair, teeth, eyes: all contain protein and are maintained and rebuilt with protein. Fats and carbohydrates are your body's oil and gasoline, they are burned together to produce energy. Vitamins and minerals are its spark plugs, essential to the utilization of food and its assimilation into the blood stream. It is a marvelously sturdy motor car, this body of yours - marvelous in its ability to maintain and rebuild itself. Given care, consideration, and respect, it will function smoothly. Neglected or abused and it will break down. Scientists are unanimous in agreeing that over-nutrition, through excess calories stored as fat, can contribute materially to physical deterioration."

B. THE IMPORTANCE OF PROPER DIET AND NUTRITION TO COMPETITIVE SHOOTERS.

The army trains men to be winners. Winners in combat and winners in any competitive activity. If the pistol competitor falters, his energy exhausted, it must not be because of a diet deficient in essential nutrients.

Proper nutrition will assure strength and endurance to perform your job well. Your job is to shoot championship scores in every match fired all day long, not just the first match or two of the day.

The expert marksman must feel well and be energetic to shoot well. No stone can be left unturned in today's level of competition that will provide that important "edge" that may be the narrow margin of victory.

Good nutrition is based on a diet that includes all the essential nutrients. These nutrients are found in a wide range of foods.

C. THE ESSENTIAL NUTRIENTS.

The essential nutrients are Protein, Fat, Carbohydrates, and protective ingredients or Vitamins.

1. Proteins are the body's building blocks. As the house builder uses various building materials to construct a house, proteins build and replace the body's tissue of muscle, nerves, tendons and all of the vital organs, etc. This is done in the form of amino acids. For instance, the lining of the gastro-intestinal tract is renewed every three days.

2. The protein built body must have fuel to consume as it moves about and also take care of the energy demands of the vital body functions. The body maintains a reserve of energy by converting fats to glucose and storing it in the liver.

Fats and fatty acids are the long range source of energy. The fat in the diet provides the full gas tank reserve for endurance. Part of the fatty acids are converted to easily digested sugar forms that are stored in the liver. The fatty acids that are not held in reserve in the liver provide for part of the present energy needs of the body or they are deposited in and about the muscular system. The complete absence of fat in the diet means slow starvation even if the other nutrients are ample.

3. There is another source of energy but a smaller portion of the amount eaten goes into the ready reserve.

Carbohydrates are the high octane energy source. Compare fats and carbohydrates to the relative combustion qualities of oil and gasoline respectively. Both will burn but gasoline is ignited easier and burns quicker. Starches and basic sugars are converted into a more readily useable glucose at a relatively faster rate than fats. In this form, they are absorbed by the blood system and supplied to the muscular tissue to furnish needed energy.

For example: Alcohol, a starch food, can pass through the entire gastro-intestinal tract without being altered in any way and yet be absorbed readily. There is no question about the energetic effect it has on some people.

4. Vitamins aid the breakdown of nutrients into useable forms. Protective ingredients or vitamins are not considered to be a food but they are essential to proper nutrition. Vitamins are a means of triggering the chemical reactions that convert the essential nutrients into useable forms in the digestive process. For example, the automble carbureator converts gasoline from a liquid into a more useable form of a vapor of gasoline molecules mixed with a large proportion of air.

D. TYPES OF FOOD THAT SUPPLY NEEDED NUTRITION.

The pistol shooter can be assured of receiving the important elements of nutrition in his diet if certain representative foods of each type are known to him.

1. There are three foods that are the main source of protein in the diet.

Proteins are mainly supplied by eggs, meat and milk. A shooter of 140 pounds should consume 100-120 grams of protein in his daily diet. Approximately one half should come from the animal source foods; eggs, meat and milk. The remaining amount can be obtained from the usual sources of bread and vegetables.

2. The same basic foods provide a source for another essential nutrient, fat.

Fats or fatty acids are obtained from animal fats and vegetable oils. The average shooter consumes too much fat. While in training, a 140 pound man should consume 70 to 90 grams of fat daily. Half of this amount should come from animal sources such as eggs, meat and milk. The remainder should come from vegetable oil sources such as peanuts, corn, soya and olives. Moderation in the use of fats is especially beneficial to the digestive process.

3. There are two main sources of carbohydrates.

Carbohydrates in the form of starches and sugar are contained in nearly all foods. It is important to give preference to such starch and sugar sources such as dark bread, fresh fruit, un-polished rice, milk, oatmeal, fresh vegetables and potatoes with the jackets on, because of the high content of protective ingredients or vitamins. Stay away from that enormous birthday cake with its gleaming white icing!

E. VITAMINS.

1. Protective ingredients or vitamins are found in most foods. In addition the human body manufactures some vitamines but usually in amounts too small to meet its needs. Some vitamins cannot be stored in the body and must be replenished daily. Vitamin pills which contain a minimum adult requirement of most identifiable vitamins should be taken only on the advice of a doctor. Your diet may be furnishing all the vitamins you need.

2. The best source of vitamins are foods in which they are naturally present. Of special importance to the shooter are the following vitamins and sources:

a. Vitamin A; is found in carrots, spinach, sweet potatoes, milk, liver, egg yolk and green and yellow vegetables. This vitamin builds resistance to the infection and helps the eyes to function normally in light of varying intensity. This feature is an aid in night vision. Vitamin A prevents and cures pellagra, a disease of the eyes and skin.

b. Vitamin B1; found in yeast, most meats, especially beef and pork, whole grain cereals, beans, peas, nuts and green vegetables. A deficiency of this vitamin causes great and persistent fatigue aching leg muscles and bones and illness of the nervous system. Vitamin B1, prevents and cures bere-beri, primarily a disease of the nervous system. Chronic alcoholics sometimes develop symptoms of the disease because alcohol diminishes the appetite and they fail to receive proper nourishment.

71

c. Vitamin C; the body does not store this vitamin and it must be replenished daily. It is found in citrus fruits, tomatoes, raw cabbage, strawberries and cantaloupe. Vitamin C promotes a healthy circulatory system, which is important to body energy; develops good sound bones, and teeth. This vitamin prevents and cures scurvy, a disease known by general listlessness and fatigue; sore, inflamed gums and various other dental disorders.

d. Vitamin D; is a fat-soluable vitamin that prevents rickets. It becomes active when exposed to ultraviolet rays. Two variations of this vitamin are important in nutrition. One is vitamin D supplied by plants. The other, vitamin D3, is found in fish-liver oils, irradiated milk, and in all irradiated animals proteins. Scientists believe that vitamin D3 forms in the skin when the body is exposed to sunlight. Because of this it has been called the "sunshine vitamin." Doctors have found that lack of vitamin D leads to serious bone changes. However, they have found that excessive amounts also cause serious bone changes.

e. Vitamin E; is a fat-soluble substance that scientists believe may be necessary for reproduction. All the functions of this vitamin are not known. The best sources of Vitamin E are wheat-germ oil and lettuce. Whole-grain cereals, meat, milk, eggs, liver, and most vegetables also contain it.

f. Vitamin K includes a group of fat-soluble vitamins that are essential for making the blood clot. These vitamins are rather abundant in food. They are found particularly in the green leafy vegetables such as spinach, cabbage, kale, and cauliflower. Pork liver is also an excellent source. Intestinal bacteria manufacture vitamin K in the body. Therefore, deficiencies of this vitamin are rarely the result of poor diet. But deficiences can result when something interferes with the normal function of the intestinal tract.

g. Certain minerals, including iron, copper, sulfur, calcium, phosphorus, iodine, and sodium, are needed for growth and to maintain tissues and regulate body functions.

E. YOU MUST HAVE STAMINA AND READY ENERGY TO BE A CHAMPION.

The lack of forceful energy to carry on under a prolonged condition of stress can be corrected to a degree by proper, balanced nutrition. You must select the various types of food that provide this needed energy.

A strong, well nourished body will allow sustained physical and mental effort under the stress of competitive shooting.

Last years beginner can become the champion this year if he learns to eat the foods that will supply him with the stamina to keep up the fight, regardless of the odds against his winning the match.

CHAPTER X

EFFECTS OF ALCOHOL, COFFEE, TOBACCO AND DRUGS

A. GENERAL

The habitual use of alcohol, coffee, tobacco and various drugs is harmful to the average person and in no way promotes better body function. We can be easily fooled by misleading advertisements into believing that such things are helpful. For example, an advertisement may tell us that cigarettes are an aid to digestion. Cigarette smoking after meals does cause the saliva to flow more freely and the heart to beat faster, aiding digestion. But, this may also result in overwork for the salivary glands and the heart. In like manner, many people may believe that a highball or cocktail at the beginning of a meal promotes digestion because of the greater flow of the digestive juices that alcohol causes. And what about that change of pace drink, tea? It is no different in caffeine content than coffee but possesses increased amounts of tannic acid.

1. Inform yourself. Any drug which causes the body organs to perform their work at a greater rate than normal, fatigues them sooner and causes them to age more rapidly. Stimulants and depressants overwork many vital organs, often when their best performance is needed for normal body activity. The effects of the use of such substances depend upon how much is used and whether or not the body is strong enough to repair the damage done.

2. In order to understand the discussion that follows there are certain terms whose specific meaning you should know. A stimulant is a chemical which, when taken into the body, excites the organs to greater effort. Depressants are chemicals which slow down body action but may also speed up body functions by reducing the influence of the nerve centers which slow down body action. For example, nicotine increases heart action by depressing the nerves that slow the heart beat, thus causing a faster pulse. Depressants deaden pain and lessen discomfort and thus make us feel better without removing the cause.

3. Much has been written and said both pro and con concerning the habitual use of alcohol, coffee, tobacco, and drugs, their temporary and permanent effects on the human body, both mental and physical. Material covering these subjects is available at any well stocked library. Part of the information that follows was derived from this source but much of the evidence against alcohol, coffee, tobacco and drugs that we are concerned with has been contributed by the shooters themselves.

a. Although all shooters are not in agreement that complete abstinence by habitual users is the solution, all will agree that these agents will in no way help to improve shooting performance or scores.

b. To learn the fundamentals of pistol shooting is no great achievement in itself. Anyone interested in becoming a pistol shooter can with persistency and training learn to shoot with some degree of proficiency. What then, is necessary to become a skilled shooter? The top shooters in the nation today unanimously agree that control is the most important factor in becoming a top competitor. Control can best be explained as the coordination of mental and physical effort, born in thought and culminating in a concentrated, precise action. This effort must be natural, unstrained, and smooth flowing. Any habit or action that results in departure from perfect coordination will lessen the degree of control and reduce the effectiveness of the action. In shooting, lessening of control shows itself in lower scores and poor performance.

c. What can you the shooter do about sustaining control? The same thing you would do when training for a match. When you find yourself having difficulty in maintaining your shot groups in the center of the target, you analyze and make corrections, be it position, grip or sight adjustment, etc. Sometimes when control is declining, analysis may pinpoint some cause other than faulty technique in employment of the fundamentals. What did you have at breakfast? Coffee - two cups and two cigarettes. Enough to ruin anyone's control. Perhaps a few too many last night and a loss of several hours of sleep. Whatever the reasons, they should be noted in your scorebook just as you would enter unusual conditions at a match. In a short period of time, if you are honest with yourself you will be able to piece together enough information upon which to take remedial action. The most difficult person to convince is yourself. No one who habitually smokes or drinks coffee wants to admit that such habits have the effect of destroying control. So they remain slaves to habits which in affect they attempt to overpower by mental and physical exertion, often ending in frustration and exhaustion.

The following paragraphs cover the effects that alcohol, coffee, tobacco and drugs have on control of pistol shooting. If you have been plagued with a built-in error, it may be that the answer to your problems lies herein.

B. ALCOHOL (ETHER)

1. <u>Effects of alcohol on the human body:</u>

The name alcohol is used for a number of organic substances some of which, like glycerin, are necessary to good health. The scientific name for the alcohol sold for drinking purposes is ethyl alcohol. Ethyl alcohol is generally considered to be a habit forming narcotic. However, in the strictest scientific sense it is an anesthetic or pain killer like ether, which is made from it.

a. Alcohol taken into the body passes through the walls of the stomach and the small intestine and thence into the blood stream. It is rapidly distributed through the body and promptly affects the brain by decreasing its ability to take up oxygen. Even a small percentage of alcohol in the blood may sometimes cause remarkable effects. Inhibitions and the corresponding cautions are removed, reactions are slowed, coordination is impaired. The senses become less acute, particularly that of sight. The field of vision is reduced - ordinary objects become darker and indistinct - poorly lighted objects are lost entirely. Reactions are slowed down and concentration becomes difficult.

b. A peculiar property of ethyl alcohol is its ability to take up water. It is a valuable dehydrating and preserving agent. When used as a drink, alcohol produces a burning sensation as it takes up water from the delicate mucous membranes of the throat, stomach, and intestines, thus causing the drinker to become thirsty. Once alcohol becomes a part of the blood, its dehydrating properties are much reduced.

c. Although alcohol is a source of heat energy, its depressing effect upon the nerve centers that control the size of blood vessels causes the blood vessels of the skin to enlarge. So long as alcohol remains in the blood to affect the brain, extra heat loss by radiation will take place through the skin and prevent any benefit that might be derived from its oxidation and the resulting warmth. For this reason, in severely cold weather, the man who drinks whisky to keep warm is in much greater danger of freezing than the person who does not.

2. <u>Effects of Alcohol on Shooting:</u>

a. Contrary to popular belief, alcohol acts as a depressant rather than a stimulant. It dulls the senses, lessens the desire to win, destroys coordination and lessens the shooter's ability to concentrate. Alcohol taken at the proper time in the proper amount might possibly lessen the shooter's anxiety but by doing so other effects are released that are far more harmful to the body and detrimental to the shooter's score. No one can say what the right amount is or when it should be taken. Some shooters may shoot a good score with a hangover. But, the second day is when the after affects become acutely noticeable and the shooter's control may disintegrate on the firing line.

b. Experimental research scientists using delicate tests and sensitive instruments, have been able to demonstrate the adverse effect of even small amounts of alcohol on various isolated bodily functions such as sensory perception and discrimination, reaction time, fine coordination, judgment, alertness and efficiency of dexterity. The changes observed have no apparent difference in quality, magnitude or expression from those due to fatigue, hunger, distraction and a host of other environmental factors. These facts establish that one small drink of intoxicating beverage places the shooter under an enormous handicap. The false feeling of well-being is deceptive. Alcohol, and gun powder do not mix.

C. COFFEE (Caffeine)

What's wrong with drinking coffee? That is easy - caffeine. Each cup contains an amount equal to about two pinches of salt. That doesn't sound like much, until you realize that it is one-third of the amount given by doctors as a heart stimulant. With three cups of coffee you are getting a dose of caffeine calculated by scientists to be medically effective for making a weakened heart work as hard and fast as a normal heart. When a heart is ready to quit, and won't pump another beat without the help of caffeine, maybe such a measure is justified. Are you sure your heart is ready for a synthetic jolt three to six times a day?

1. Effects of Coffee on the Human Body: Many coffee drinkers say they can't do without it as a pick-me-up during the day. But let us see what really happens after that coffee break. Dr. Rolf Ulrich, in his book, "Coffee and Caffeine," reports that after coffee consumption, mental tempo rises first, and speed of association increases, but there is a noticeable decrease in the quality of work being done. In test examinations it was seen that the subjects finished quicker, but that false conclusions were more frequent. Reliability and accuracy definitely took a beating as a result of a coffee pep-up.

The physical result is the same. Caffeine raises muscular output temporarily, but in severe physical demands of longer duration, the muscular output decreases. As a famous scientist has said. "Coffee acts like a spur, which drives a horse to do its best, but cannot replace oats." That is the whole problem in humans - many of them do expect coffee to take the place of "oats." They pass up a solid breakfast because they can get by with coffee. The stimulating and exhilerating affects coffee produces is usually followed by a loss of energy and a feeling of unsteadiness. No matter how we look at it, coffee takes more from the body than it gives. All coffees contain caffeine but in varying amounts. Fresh ground coffee is the most potent in caffeine. Instant coffees contain half as much and decaffeineated coffees contain about one third as much. It is imperative that a shooter refrain from drinking coffee before and during the shooting session and be moderate in coffee consumption when not firing.

2. Are you considering a change of pace drink, like tea? Before you do, read the following:

It is not generally known that tea has larger amounts of caffeine and tannic acid (the two most detrimental ingredients) per weight, than coffee. Caffeine in tea leaves is about three percent in ratio of one to two percent in coffee. The general effects of caffeine are cerebral, cardiac and dieretic (copious urination) stimulation. As to tannic acid, tea leaves have about ten percent while coffee berries have only about five percent content. Tannic acid, when brought into contact with mucuous membrance, acts as an astrigent and dimishes its secretions. It coagulates albuminous substances and thus hardens animal source food matter in the stomach with which it comes in contact. It also leads to more rapid clotting of the blood when absorbed into blood circulation. There is evidence of liver damage from extensive use. In solution, it is unstable and should not come in contact with metals. Since coffee is made about twice as strong as tea in liquid form, a strong cupful of either will contain about two grains of caffeine and over three grains of tannic acid.

3. A shooter should stay away from the colas. Cola drinks, in addition to other soft drinks, contain that well known perk-up ingredient, caffeine. The bottles of some brands contain a listing of cola contents which should serve as a reminder. Know them and avoid them while shooting.

D. TOBACCO (Nicotine)

For a period after January 1964 when the U. S. Surgeon General (see paragraph D3, this chapter) revealed to the American public the results of an investigation into cigarette smoking and health, many smokers quit the habit. At the end of one year a poll taken revealed that one out of every four hundred smokers had quit. This small percentage points up the fact that most smokers will continue the habit no matter what the future consequences might be. The smoking habit is easily acquired and even after a short duration becomes a difficult habit to break. For this reason one who has not yet acquired the habit should be encouraged to abstain. The objective of this section is to provide you the shooter with information that will enable you to establish control of smoking in order to improve your shooting. Who knows, once you gain control of the smoking habit and can turn it on or off at will you might be inspired to quit all together.

1. The Effects Tobacco has on the Human Body. Nicotine is a powerful alkaloid poison. Its chemical formula in $C10H14N2$, which means that it contains carbon, hydrogen, and nitrogen in the proportions indicated by the numbers.

a. Being a volatile substance, it is carried along with the burning smoke of the tobacco. In cigarettes about 61 percent of the nicotine is burned and destroyed, 27 percent is ordinarily exhaled, and about 12 percent is absorbed by the smoker. The absorbed nicotine specifically affects the nerves that regulate the heart rate and the size of the blood vessels, and, therefore, alters the pulse rate and the blood pressure. For about ten minutes after smoking is begun, the pulse rate is slowed about five beats per minute because of an increased stimulation of the nerves that slow the heart beat. After this temporary slowing effect, nicotine depresses these same nerves. This results in an increased pulse rate that lasts for two or three hours. The increase, for the average person, is from five to ten extra beats per minute. One cigarette after breakfast will step up heart beat for half the shooting day. With the damage already done, abstaining for the rest of the day's shooting is to small avail. The work of the heart is affected not only by the increased pulse rate but also by the decrease in size of the arteries. Both of these factors raise blood pressure and increase the work of the heart.

b. The carbon monoxide which is also present in tobacco smoke will, if inhaled, reduce the capacity of the hemoglobin of the red corpuscles to carry oxygen. This is due to the fact that hemoglobin absorbs carbon monoxide about 300 times faster than it does oxygen with which it ordinarily combines. Therefore, to the extent that the blood takes on carbon monoxide it cannot in that same proportion, carry oxygen. This results in "cutting the wind, " or breathlessness, whenever there is exertion.

c. In 1959, the American Cancer Society began a study to prove that there exists an association between cigarette smoking and many physical complaints. The study involved 1,079,000 men and women (smokers and nonsmokers.) For comparison purposes we have listed five of the more important complaints:

COMPLAINT	CIG. SMOKERS	NON-SMOKERS
Cough	33. 2%	5. 6%
Loss of appetite	3. 3%	0. 6%
Shortness of breath	16. 3%	4. 7%
Easily fatigued	26. 1%	14. 9%
Loss of weight	7. 3%	4. 5%

One can readily see that the complaints were more prevalent among the cigarette smokers than non-smokers. The study further revealed that lung functioning is affected if one inhales cigarette smoke regardless of age. For example: A young man who smokes one pack of cigarettes per day has the same efficiency of lung functioning of a man 20 years senior to him who does not smoke.

2. Effects of Tobacco on Shooting:

a. The combined effects of nicotine and carbon monoxide explain why the pistol shooter must avoid smoking if he is to shoot with the greatest possible skill. This conclusion does not mean that an individual or a team whose members smoke may not win, if it is competing against inferior opponents, but it does mean that any individual shooter on a team cannot perform at his best if he uses tobacco. The top competition today does not allow a margin of indulgence if you expect to win. Denying yourself a quick drag on the weed is not a sacrifice, it is a necessity for victory.

b. Simply explained, cigarette smoking affects the smoker by:

(1) Initially, slowing the pulse rate.

(2) Increasing the pulse rate.

(3) Increasing blood pressure and overworking the heart.

(4) Reducing the oxygen capacity of the blood, causing shortness of breath.

(5) Bringing on fatigue more quickly.

c. From the standpoint of shooting, smoking does affect performance, and more importantly, control. It is possible to become more proficient in shooting and still continue smoking, but the road is long and the progress slow. Many of our top shooters can attest to that fact. Today most of the determination to reach the top was stronger than the addiction to tobacco. Occasionally, you may see one sport a cigar, but seldom, if ever, will you see one inhale tobacco smoke. Consequently, the crux of the problem of smoking is the inhalation of tobacco smoke. Herein lies the answer. Stop inhaling and you have solved the problem. It is the inhaled nicotine and carbon monoxide that are responsible for upsetting the normal body balance. For this reason we find many shooters making the switch from cigarettes to pipes and cigars, since the smoke of each is generally too toxic for the normal person to inhale. Performance as well as health improves accordingly. For the shooter who will consider quitting, we offer a plan, entitled "You Can Quite Smoking," paragraph D4, this chapter. Mark Twain once said that he had no difficulty giving up smoking, and added "I have done it a thousand times." If you decide though, make it permanent.

3. <u>The report of the Surgeon General of the US Public Health Service</u>, released on 11 January 1964.

"SMOKERS DIE EARLY" it says, "Smoking cigarettes is a health hazard that calls for corrective action - and is a major cause of lung cancer and other death-dealing diseases, especially in men," a blue-ribbon federal panel reported.

In short, the panel indicated, the more you smoke, the greater your risk of an early death. Deeply inhaled cigarette smoke sends a threat of premature death spreading through the lungs, arteries and the heart itself.

a. Lung tissue was obtained from more than 1000 postmortems, put on microscope slides and carefully examined by pathologists. The slides were indentified only with coded numbers, and pathologists did not know their origin. Later, statiticians matches the pathological findings with the histories of the dead patients. The results added up to an elaborate description of progressive smoke damage.

b. Deeply inhaled smoke, the researchers found, irritates the cells that line the tiniest chambers of the lung (alveoli). The walls of the alveoli thicken, lose their elasticity and much of their ability to do their vital job of exchanging carbon dioxide for oxygen. Subjected to sudden stress--such as a cough or sneeze--the alveolar walls rupture; a minute part of the lung becomes useless.

c. Even while it is attacking the alveoli, smoke also damages the small arteries that carry blood to the interior lung surfaces for oxygenation. The artery walls become fibrous and thickened. Soon, internal deposits on the thickened walls make the arteries so narrow that little blood can get through. Eventually many tiny arteries are blocked completely.

These two sets of events alone would be enough to explain why thousands of Americans are "lung cripples," suffering from what most U. S. Doctors call pulmonary fibrosis and chronic emphysema. But the damaging chain of events runs on.

d. The destruction of smaller blood vessels in the lung and the thickening of slightly larger ones increases the blood pressure in the pulmonary arteries and puts a strain on the right side of the heart. It also prompts the left side of the heart to work harder to pump blood against increased resistance. A healthy heart could probably stand the extra work; a heart already weakened by other difficulties might fail.

e. Even while the heart is being asked to overexert, carbon monoxide from cigarette smoke combines with red blood cells decreases their capacity to carry oxygen. As a result, the hardworking heart muscle is given less fuel to do its job. At the same time, tobacco's nicotine causes a constriction of small arteries in the extremities and speeds up the heart, increasing its need for oxygen and complicating the coronary problem.

f. Smoking dulls the sense of taste causing loss of appetite, thus creating a loss of weight. For this reason people who give up smoking tend to stop losing weight. They begin to taste food again and enjoy eating.

4. <u>You Can Quit Smoking!</u>

a.   A vicious, velvety trap; Light a cigarette, smoke it, taste its bitterness, put it out.
Even as you do, you know that you will want another. Not that you enjoy it. You simply want it. and
why?

(1) When you smoke a cigarette, for instance, nicotine, carbon monoxide, small
amount of hydrocyanic acid, pyridine and various phenols and aldehydes are absorbed into your lungs
and mouth. Your nervous system is momentarily stimulated. Your blood pressure goes up. Your
pulse rate increases.

(2) Most important of all to the satisfaction of the habitual smoker, your blood vessels
undergo a constriction. This "slows you down. " That is, after the momentary stimulation, smoking
depresses, for a far longer period.

(3) When you smoke, you are artificially slowing down most of your body's normal
activities. If you are suddenly confronted with an emotional psychological emergency: adrenalin is
pumped into your blood stream, your muscles tense, you breathe faster and get edgy, jittery--"nervous. " Tobacco smoke retards these natural processes by slowing the blood circulation and thus "calm-
ing you down. " You find a smoke is "good for your nerves. "

(4) If you smoke a pack and a half of cigarettes a day, you smoke an average of one
cigarette every 32 minutes of your waking hours. That many crises don't arise every day. You need
cigarettes simply because your body has come to expect this depressant effect every so often. You begin consciously to want to cigarette.

(5) There is little true pleasure in smoking. The harsh taste, the hot dryness is
tolerated, for the sake of tobacco's mild narcotic effect. If it were possible for you to go without cigarettes for the next 24 hours, and then light one, you would find out how distasteful and noxious tobacco
smoke really is. If you think this is an exaggeration, try it.

(6) Think back to the time many years ago when you smoked your first cigarette. How
did it taste? Gaseous, strong, biting, wasn't it? This is the experience that you may give your system
30 to 60 times a day. You are able to do it because the human mechanism is a marvelously adjustable
piece of machinery which can get used to almost anything.

b.   What can you do about it? You have already taken one big step toward giving up smoking: you have been thinking about the detrimental effects of smoking and about giving it up. If you want
to stop smoking, think about giving it up at one fell swoop. Think of it cooly and calmly, without fear
or hopelessness. Think of what it would be like to never have to smoke. Giving up smoking isn't all
self-denial; there are compensations. There are so many good things to enjoy more when you give
yourself a chance to fully appreciate them. You will never want to go back to smoking.

(1) When you give up smoking, your food will taste much better. Your nose and throat
and lungs will not be continuously permeated with smoke. You will begin to smell the world around you.
When you walk into a garden you will smell as well as see the flowers. When you get up in the morning,
you won't find your throat clogged with phlegm, and you won't cough or clear your throat so often.

(2) You will actually feel far less nervous. That is hard to believe--for during the
first days of non-smoking you will be nervous. The depressant effect smoking has exerted on your body
for years suddenly ends, and the unfamiliar effect is almost overwhelming. You will possibly be more
emotional; you may laugh at trival things and, for a while, be tense, jumpy. But gradually the nervousness diminishes. You will be calmer, more poised. For when you stop slowing down your body and
cutting your energy with tobacco, you will find that you have much more energy. There will be more
time to get things done.

(3) A word of caution here. It is generally believed that a reformed smoker gains
weight. If you have trouble with your waistline, remember this: when you stop smoking, you will not
gain more than a few pounds. When you stop smoking, you will have a great increase in energy. In using up that energy, you will burn away a lot of the weight that you would otherwise put on.

(4) If you have read this far, you probably think you are about ready to swear off.
Don't do it yet.

c. To stop smoking, follow these rules:

(1) Watch and wait until some time when your life is on a fairly even keel. Don't try it when you are leaving on an important trip, or preparing to give a big party, or when you are facing some personal emergency. Don't postpone it too long, either, or you will lose the momentum you are gradually building up.

(2) But some sunny morning--maybe on a weekend--you will wake up feeling especially good. You will have had a good night's sleep; you will feel fit for anything. The idea of stopping smoking will pop into your head. Why foul up a wonderful day with the noxious fumes of burning tar and nicotine? Decide, then and there quietly and firmly, that you are through with smoking! This is the moment, intelligently selected and properly prepared for, when you can get off with a running start.

(3) After you have started yourself off with as much momentum as you can, tell your friends that you have given up smoking. Don't be smug or complacent or boastful, but let people know what you are doing. Then, at some point when you are seriously tempted to smoke, the thought of all the derisive laughter you will get for giving in may well carry you over the crisis.

(4) Most smokers have fixed ideas about the occasions when a smoke tastes best. The first cigarette after breakfast, or the one with a cocktail before dinner. If such associations are likely to tempt you to smoke, brace yourself in advance for such temptations; tell yourself that such an occasion is coming, and that you must be prepared to want to smoke badly. If you hold out only for a moment, that sudden strong temptation will die almost as quickly as it arose.

(5) Don't permit yourself to make a single exception. Until the non-smoking habit is firmly implanted, "don't." If a habit is not fed, it dies relatively quickly, but it can subsist for a long time on the slightest food. If you occasionally let yourself have one cigarette or pipe on the ground that "just one won't hurt," you will keep alive the desire to smoke. Just one drink is too many for an alcoholic, as one cigarette is too many for the heavy smoker who is trying to reform. Win the battle of the moment--every time you say no to the temptation to smoke, you are making the next "no" easier.

(6) Baby yourself to an extent. Most of us are inclined to launch sudden, ambitious programs of self-improvement. We try to do more than we can resonably expect of ourselves. On the contrary, indulge yourself a little. Eat what you want and enjoy it. Make it a habit to carry mints, gum, or salted nuts. During the first few weeks keep substitutes on hand--and pop one into your mouth whenever you feel like smoking.

(7) Let your sleep work for you. On the night of the first day that you give up smoking, think for a moment when you go to bed of how today you did not smoke. Then tell yourself, "Tomorrow I am not going to smoke." Repeat it to yourself as you get drowsy. This will be the last thing in your conscious mind as you drop off to sleep. When you wake in the morning, remind yourself that you are going to get through this day, too, without smoking. Don't make a big issue of it; just briefly say: "This day I don't smoke." Even if you don't follow the other rules set down here, this exercise in "controlled sleep" could get you over the hump. You will find a sense of freedom and independance and self-assurance results from simply going half a day without tobacco. This is a sharp, continuing pleasure, and every minute helps to strengthen you against the next minute's temptation. Above and beyond this pleasant, heartening knowledge is the awareness that you are doing something of which you will be proud--not to mention healthier and happier--for the rest of your life. Six months or six years from now, when someone offers you a cigarette, you will refuse it, but not weakly or defensively. You will say "Thanks--I use to smoke, but I gave it up."

5. Expense: If a man smokes two packs of cigarettes a day for 365 days it will cost him $290.00 a year! Quit smoking and automatically you save money, remain healthy, and start winning pistol matches. This is a bargain you can't afford to overlook.

E. DRUGS

At one time or another some shooters have probably tried a sedative drug or tranquilizer to see what effects it would have on their shooting. Drugs affect different people in different ways, so dosage would be a problem even if they did any good toward reducing anxiety, nervousness, etc. Any time medication or drugs are used that affect the body functions, there is a change that the side effects will do more harm than good to the shooter's performance.

Some shooters no doubt prescribe certain remedies for themselves when they have a cold, a stopped-up nose or a headache. Here are some of the effects of the drugs found in these and other preparations. Most of the effects are not conductive to good shooting. Most drugs are habit forming and all are a deterrant to good health if used frequently without proper medical advice. There is not substitute for good clean living, a healthy body and just plain GUTS!

1. A depressant slows reflexes, lessens the desire to win, promotes carelessness, causes loss of concentration and coordination.

2. A stimulant causes nervousness, hypertension, increases heartbeat, excessive movement of the hands, trembling, etc.

3. Drugs in daily use.

a. Barbiturates. (To induce rest and sleep)

Phenobarbital has special effects against insomnia. Continued use increases tolerance and leads to dependence. Acute anxiety may result if the drug is abruptly discontinued after long use. Alcoholics substitute barbiturates for alcohol and become just as devoted to it. Even after moderate doses, lassitude, dizziness, headache, nausea and diarrhea may occur. Other toxic effects are respiratory depressions peripheral vascular collapse, feeble heart beat, low body temperature and continued stupor with depressed reflexes.

b. Analgesics (Pain relief and reduction of symptomatic discomfort)

Aspirin - acetylsalicylic acid (relief of headache, fever and other symtomatic discomfort).

Gastro-intestinal distress due to irritation is common. Continued dosage symptoms same as quinine (Cinchonism): Dizziness, ringing in ears, impaired hearing, acidosis and depressed blood clotting mechanism.

c. Stimulants or adrenergics (Relief from drowsiness, depression, curbing the appetite and relief from nasal congestion.)

Benzedrine, amphetamine and ephedrine elevate blood pressure, accelerate the heart beat, causes headaches, nervousness, insomnia and spasms of the urinary bladder's sphincter. (Muscular control that permits urination.)

d. Antihistamines (Relief of colds and fever and relief or prevention of allergy symptoms.)

Exerts a potent sedative effect. There is a danger of toxic action, especially drowsiness. A form of antihistamine namely, methapyrilene, is used for sedative purposes. Used in conjunction with alcohol, this sedative action is especially dangerous as alcohol heightens the depressant effect.

e. APC pills: (Relief of headache and other symptomatic discomfort) Basic ingredients usually are acetanlid or acetophentidin and caffeine. Continued use develops a blood condition known as methemoglobinemia or simply a union of oxygen and iron in the blood instead of oxygen and hemoglobin, the natural state. The oxygen in this instance is retained in the blood and not exchanged normally. Another combination used is aspirin (acetylsalicylic acid), phenacetin and caffeine. The phenacentin adds the property of antipyretic (reduction of fever.) Other effects similar to above.

f. Decongestant tables. (Relief of colds, fever and prevention of allery symptoms). Basic ingredients quite similar, usually as follows:

(1) Phenylephrine hydrodoride. A stimulant of the sympathomimetic group. It is a local vaso-contrictor, elevates blood pressure, reduces swelling of nasal membranes. It is usually mixed with a local anesthetic to retard rate of absorption. Used in treatment of vasomotor collapse which is a condition where the nervous system cannot control the dilation and contraction of the blood vessels.

(2) Phenindamine tartrate. An antihistamine. The tartaric acid may be detrimental to the kidneys.

(3) Acelylsalicyclic acid (aspirin). See aspirin described above.

(4) An antipyretic (reduce fever) and analygesic.

(5) Caffeine. A stimulant, produces wakefulness and respiratory stimulation. When combined with an analgesic it is used to relieve headache. Continued use may produce nervousness and insomnia.

(6) Vitamin "C," (ascorbic acid): large dosage leads to gastro-intestinal upset.

SECTION FOUR

INTERNATIONAL PISTOL PROGRAM

INTERNATIONAL PISTOL COMPETITION

Competitive shooting is taking on a very important role in the field of International relationships. As interested parties both in shooting and in our national interests, we must strive to carry our flag to the winner's platform in the Olympics, Pan American Games, World Games, etc.

One of our goals in International type shooting is to bring to light the valuable nature of International competition. It has become obvious that with the progressive improvement in communications and transportation media, our lives are becoming more and more influenced and effected psychologically speaking, by the actions of our neighbors throughout the world. Ideas concerning speech, clothing, religion, and sometimes our politics are influenced by our neighbors. No less can be said of sporting events. If we are to exert influence upon our rivals overseas in the international shooting field and gain their respect, we have a major task: Win in International competition. Everyone listens to a winner!

Those shooters who have competed in International competition can testify to the far reaching International good-will engendered by the personal relationships enjoyed with individual shooters from other countries. Even the most hardbitten personality thaws to a degree when he performs well in an event in which individuals of other nations are competing. There is an element of warmth in the sharing of feelings experienced by each contestant which promotes better understanding and many times generates lasting friendships.

The International Rapid Fire course provides the pistol shooter with challenges in time and targets that he has never faced before. This type of shooting is especially interesting to those shooters who have become proficient in NRA type rapid fire shooting and are looking for something more demanding.

The International Center Fire course challenges such a wide scope of competitors that it has almost universal appeal. The weapons used are basically the same as those used in the Center Fire NRA Course.

The International Slow Fire is one of the most difficult challenges a pistol shooter can face. This type of shooting is especially interesting to those shooters who have become proficient in the NRA type slow fire shooting and are looking for wider fields of endeavor.

By becoming involved in International type firing, you have an opportunity to determine the skill level required to earn a berth on United States Teams in the next World Games, Pan American Games or Olympic competitions.

International shooting demands a higher degree of control than that found in any type of domestic competition that you may have experienced. Learn, and employ this higher degree of control in your shooting and win yourself a place on the U.S. International Shooting Team.

The International Shooting Union (ISU) is the sponsoring and controlling organization for all authorized International Pistol Matches. This organization is also known in most other countries as the Union Internationale De Tiro (UIT) with headquarters in Weisbaden, West Germany.

CHAPTER XI

INTERNATIONAL SLOW FIRE

1. The ISU Slow Fire, 50 Meter Pistol competition is fired with the Free Pistol. Ten sighting shots and 60 competition shots at 50 meters are fired in six series of ten shots in a time limit of three hours. The possible score is 600 points. Competitors are permitted to fire the sighting shots before or between ten-shot string. Shots may be marked in the pits or by the Register Keeper, who is stationed behind the firing point. The Register Keeper may determine the estimated value of each shot with the aid of a telescope. Official scoring will be done by the Official Scorer after firing is completed.

2. An international slow fire pistol range shall comprise a line of targets, normally so mounted that they can be changed during competition without interrupting the shooting or disturbing the competitors. At a distance of fifty meters from the line of targets and parallel to it, there shall be a line of firing points covered by a roof and each firing point protected from the wind. The distance will be measured from the front limit of the space used by the shooters to the corresponding target. The targets must not be placed more than 75 cms above and not more than 125 cms below the level of the pistol when held in normal shooting position. Each firing point must not be more than two meters to the side of a line 90° to the targets. If the range lies open to strong winds, it is desirable to protect it by lines of trees or walls, so constructed that part of the air is allowed to pass through small openings in the walls. The protection shall not be closer than about five meters from the nearest line of fire and so that shadows are not thrown onto the targets. The International 50 meters slow fire pistol target is divided into ten circular zones, scoring from ten to one. The ten ring has an outside diameter of 50 mms. The changing of targets may be by the pits, or operated mechanically or electrically from each shooting position or from some central place.

3. It is forbidden to have the grip of the pistol extended in such a way that it might gain support from any other part of the arm than the hand. Optical sights are not allowed. The trigger weight is not specified, but it must be safe. Any caliber .22 weapon can be used for the Slow Fire Course. Generally, a Free Pistol is used.

Figure 11-1. International Free Pistol.

4. In Free Pistol shooting the arm holding the pistol must be free of support from the body. You are not allowed to wear a wrist watch or anything else that might give any support to the pistol. The shooter must adopt his position so that it is clearly visible that he does not gain any support from the wall or the bench or any other permanent or temporary structure. It is necessary to know the pistol and the technique of its use, as well as the rules and course of fire, before embarking on the difficult trip to success. The shooter's hand should feel comfortable in a custom fired grip. The shape of the grip should let him hold the pistol properly with the least possible effort. The larger the contact surface between the hand and the grips the better. It is especially advantageous to have the whole thumb base touching the grips. The hand support should reach as far to the rear as permitted. However, it must not reach behind the wrist. The adjustable trigger of the free pistol, usually has a trigger pull from 15 to 40 grams 1/2 to 1 1/2 ozs. The trigger is equipped with a trigger pull adjusting screw. Many shooters adjust the trigger as light as possible. This can produce problems because an involuntary movement may accidentally trigger the weapon before the shooter is ready. A too lightly adjusted trigger does not allow the shooter to touch the trigger when aiming. You must leave a certain amount of weight on the trigger to enable the shooter to touch and feel the trigger. This gives more security and confidence to the shooter. There are three methods of operating the free-pistol trigger:

a. The shooter puts the trigger finger lightly on the trigger immediately after having raised the arm to a shooting position and applies positive trigger pressure until the shot breaks. Usually a full setting of 1 1/2 ozs is used in this method.

b. With a lighter trigger of approximately one ounce, the shooter carefully bends his trigger finger toward the trigger making slight contact, more or less depending on the front sight's minimum movement in relation to the target. If watched from the side, the trigger finger is constantly moving, bending toward the trigger or straightening out. The task for the shooter is to choose the best moment to make contact and apply enough trigger pressure to release the shot without disturbing the sights.

c. After raising the pistol the shooter makes a more positive contact of the finger on the trigger only when the sights are perfectly aligned on the aiming area. Up to this moment the trigger finger is kept free without ever touching the trigger. This method should be applied if the trigger weight is light (1/2 oz) and the pistol fires by the slightest touch on the trigger.

5. Method a is the best. Method b has some danger in that if the pistol is involuntarily jerked or disturbed by an abrupt movement it will be a bad shot. Method c requires reflex conditioning of the arm muscles because there is a delay in reaction time after attaining correct sight alignment and the firing of the shot. Deep concentration is needed in maintaining a perfect sight alignment. It is difficult to hold the trigger finger stable on a 1/2 ounce trigger for any great length of time. This method sometimes leads to an early nervous fatigue of the shooter.

6. If the grip is not correctly shaped to the hand of the shooter, often the finger touches the trigger only after excessive bending. This is uncomfortable. Many shooters install a small screw or bent wire on the trigger which can be turned and adjusted to the most favorable position where the trigger finger can reach it. This addition to the trigger should be short and as light in weight as possible. The pressure on the wire or screw comes at an angle to the axis of the pistol bore and results in the shooter applying trigger pressure at an angle. If there is excessive tolerance in fitting in the trigger mechanism, the trigger may not function correctly.

7. Determine where the placing of the center of gravity of the pistol is best for you. It should be a little forward of the position of the middle finger, depending on the individual shooter. Some shooters put additional weight on the forend believing that the front sight can be held steadier in the rear sight notch. If the front sight has movement and is unsteady and the shooter is not satisfied with the "feel" of the pistol he must experiment in order to find the most suitable center of gravity. This is found by proper balancing of the pistol in the hand. The desirable condition is when the front sight remains as steady as possible for an extended period.

8. The weight of the free pistol requires the shooter to build up the tone of the arm muscles. The exercises used in developing the arm for NRA shooting work well for this purpose also. To fire one round, the shooter must be able to hold the pistol steady for approximately 12 to 18 seconds. In a series of ten shots the shooter might raise the arm 25 to 30 times. This requires considerable endurance of the arm and shoulder muscles. To prevent excessive muscle fatigue the shooter has to practice

frequently. The fatigue will become apparent mainly in the later portion of the course of fire. To reduce the rapid onset of muscular stress, many shooters bend their body slightly rearward, opposite to the direction of the raised arm. This altered stance helps to compensate for the weight of the extended arm and pistol. The European method of holding the free pistol is with a relaxed hand. This method of holding the pistol demands special training and self control. In NRA shooting, a loose grip tends to result in wild shots. On the other hand holding the pistol too tight causes a trembling movement of front sight. In the course of practice the shooter must find the correct tension in the muscles of his hand which gives him the most stable pistol. Usually the free pistol is fired as follows:

    a. The shooter raises his arm from the shooting bench with the loaded and cocked pistol.

    b. The trigger is set.

    c. During the first two to four seconds the arm is moving but gradually settling. The front sight stabilizes and comes to rest in the rear notch. The sights then come to rest in the aiming area as a minimum arc of movement.

    d. With decreasing movement of the pistol and the attainment of good sight alignment the finger is laid lightly on the trigger without the application of pressure.

    e. The eye observes the sight alignment and is aware of the steadiness of the hold.

    f. If the sights are perfectly aligned the trigger pressure is increased to the point at which the shot breaks.

    g. The function of the trigger finger is exacting and careful. The execution of this action is enacted with much greater precision than generally experienced in NRA type shooting.

    h. If for some reason the shot was not released at the optimum moment, the finger is taken carefully away from the trigger and the pistol is lowered to the table in order to relax the arm and hand.

9. Three hours of concentrated shooting not only tires the arm but the eyes as well. As soon as there is a diminishing efficiency of eyesight, and focus can no longer be maintained clearly, the shooter must pause for a few minutes. If the arm tires, rest it. Shooting with the free pistol requires highly developed will and great mental concentration for the duration of the shooting. Keep in mind at all times:

    a. All movement of the arm should be smooth. Putting the weapon down too hard or a slight tremor during raising the pistol may accidentally fire the shot.

    b. The shooter must be determined to press positively on the trigger and not let himself be deceived by the minor movements of the sights in the aiming area, as long as the sights are aligned.

    c. If the firing is not going well, the shooter must control himself and remain patient. He must make himself raise and lower the pistol until he is satisfied with the sight alignment before firing the shot.

    d. After a bad shot, the shooter should put the pistol on the table and rest for a few minutes. Take time to analyze the cause of the bad shot. Consider this reason when planning the next shot.

    e. The shooter must never give up. He must remember that one point could make the difference in winning or losing.

10. International Slow Fire shooting demands a higher degree of control than any type of competition you have experienced in regular NRA events. Learn to use this high degree of control in your shooting and win yourself a place on the U.S. International Slow Fire Shooting Team.

Figure 11-2. Shooting the Free Pistol (Side View).

Figure 11-3. Shooting the Free Pistol (Rear View).

86

Figure 11-4. The International Slow Fire Target (Int'l 50 Meter).

CHAPTER XII

INTERNATIONAL RAPID FIRE

1. The International Rapid Fire Course involves the firing of 20 rounds in 8 seconds, 20 rounds in 6 seconds and 20 rounds in 4 seconds at the International Rapid Fire silhouette target for a total possible score of 600 points.

2. The International Rapid Fire Range consists of a series of five silhouette targets located 25 meters from the firing line. These targets are one meter apart, center to center.

The ten ring is 10 cms x 15 cms with consecutively decreasing values of scoring rings down to the value of one.

3. The course is fired in the following manner: 2 strings, 5 rounds each fired in 8 seconds, 2 strings, 5 rounds each fired in 6 seconds and 2 strings, 5 rounds each fired in 4 seconds. This makes a half course of 30 rounds. One shot is fired at each target per string. The entire series is repeated to complete the full course of 60 rounds.

4. The pistol used is relatively unrestricted so long as it can be fitted into a box 30 cm x 15 cm x 5 cm. There is a leeway allowed of 5% in one direction. Orthopedic grips may be used so long as they do not extend beyond the wrist joint. Trigger weight is not specified, but it must be safe. Sights must be metallic. Caliber is restricted to caliber .22 rimfire with the short cartridge preferred over long rifle. Weight of the pistol with all attachments and modifications cannot exceed 1260 grams in weight.

5. Before we compete in any sport we must know the basic fundamentals of that sport and how to employ them. We are fortunate in that case in that the basic fundamentals of pistol marksmanship we have learned in NRA type shooting will also apply in International Rapid Fire. The fundamentals do not change, only the method of employment is modified to meet the needs of the course of fire.

    a. Stance is the posture of the body to provide stability and balance, allowing us to deliver a series of shots without muscular strain. Since our entire performance is closely related to stance, we must take precautions to insure that our stance is exactly the same each time.

    (1) The most important aspect of stance is the placement of the feet. The feet should be slightly farther apart than in NRA type shooting. This is because while delivering the five shot series, we move the arm across the targets. This will cause a slight and unconscious movement of the torso, rotating in the direction of the movement. Because of this movement, we must have a more stable base than where there is no arm or torso movement.

    (2) The other major difference in stance is the starting or "Ready" position of the shooting arm. The shooting arm is held at a 45° angle below the horizontal until the targets start to face.

    (3) The position of the head is also important. The head must be held erect so that your vision is out of the center of the eye. If the head is lowered or tilted back, our cone of vision becomes distorted and difficulty is experienced in maintaining sight alignment. Remember these points: The feet are spread slightly further apart, but not uncomfortably so. The shooting arm is held at a 45° angle until the targets turn, and more attention must be given to the position of the head.

    b. Position is the relationship of the body and the stance with the line of targets. In Rapid Fire, we must consider five targets instead of one.

    (1) Position, or alignment of the body to the targets is limited to a degree by the shooting rules. These rules provide for a shooting platform at least 1.5 meters wide centered in front of the target bank. A bank of targets is the five targets assigned to a firing point. For all practical purposes, the shooter should limit himself to this area so that his body is located at the same place each time in relation to the target bank.

    (2) We now are ready to align ourselves with a target preparatory to starting our series of shots.

(a) The method used by many good shooters is to assume a natural stance pointing to the last target, then swing the arm back to the first target, and lower the arm to the "Ready" position. A major advantage of this position is that it allows you to move across with less muscular effort since you are moving toward your natural position. For example, it is easier to relax a spring smoothly than it is to stretch it. A point which must be closely watched is moving the arm to the first target. Since we are holding a slight muscular tension against our natural position, our arm wants to move to the left as we raise it to the firing position.

(b) Another position favored is to align the body with the first target. This gives the advantage of complete control over the arm raising to the shooting position since it is coming to a natural position. A disadvantage is moving against muscles as we move to the subsequent targets in the series, "stretching" the spring, so to speak.

(c) An additional method would be to align the body on the center target. This method has advantages and disadvantage to a greater or lesser degree than the two previous method described.

(3) Since we must move the arm in International Rapid Fire, we turn our body away from the target at a greater angle than we would in 3-gun shooting. In American 3-gun NRA type shooting, we normally face away from the targets 40-50 degrees. In International Rapid Fire, we are more nearly 90° or at right angles from the target. This limits the arm movement to the least muscular strain. Also, from the 90° position, less tension is created on the back muscles allowing the arm a more favorable angle of swing in front of the body. Regardless of which target the shooter uses as his primary alignment target, his position must meet the requirement of allowing the body to swing on all five targets without undue muscle pull. Since there is going to be a slight amount of torso movement, disregard it. Primarily the arm must move smoothly and evenly.

c. Breath Control is as important in International Rapid Fire as it is in 3-Gun NRA shooting. We must still get a sufficient amount of air into the lungs to allow us to shoot five good, well aimed shots at five different targets. A recommended method of breath control is to inhale deeply and exhale completely two or three times just before you give the command "Ready." Inhale deeply, give command "Ready," exhale about half, hold the rest, by this time the targets are turning and at a maximum of eight seconds later you can resume normal breathing. Even though breath control is as important here as 3-gun shooting, it isn't as difficult to master.

d. Sight Alignment: Sight alignment is just as important in International Rapid Fire as in NRA Slow Fire shooting. Even though the targets are closer and the "10 ring" larger, we still cannot settle for "almost" or "half-way" sight alignment. We must strive for perfect sight alighment each and every time we press the trigger. It makes no difference if it is the first target or the last or a target in between; sight alignment is exactly the same as we are accustomed to.

(1) In explaining sight alignment in Rapid Fire, we must be conscious of several things. First is the target movement; second is the movement of the gun to the firing position; and third, the sights.

(a) Since the target movement is our signal to start our gun to target movement, we must see the target move. It is not necessary, nor is it desirable, to focus on the target while waiting for this movement. By focusing on the target, we must shift our focus to the front sight before firing. This is just something else to think about and accomplish before firing. One of the accepted methods is to fix the focus of the eye on the point in space where the sights will appear.

(b) This is determined by lifting the arm from the "Ready" position to the "Fire" position, aligning the sights with the aiming area, focusing on the front sight. Lower the arm to "Ready" Position maintaining the fixed point of focus. Give the command "Ready" and as the targets turn, raise the arm, bring the sights to this point of focus and fire. All this can be done by using what is called "the cone of vision."

(c) When do we pick up our sights and perfect the alignment? Some good shooters pick up the sights as low as the 7 or 8 ring at 6 o'clock. It is felt by most shooters, however, that the best place to pick up the sights is not lower than the nine ring and preferably in the lower part of the ten ring. By using this latter method, our focus is not shifted so far from the area where our sight alignment will be. After we have moved the arm into the "Fire" position, perfected our sight alignment, we press the trigger and prepare to move to the next target.

(2) The question arises, what about an aiming point. With the focus on the front sight, we will see three white lines on the target. Simply move the sights to the center of these white lines. Since it is natural to point to the center of mass, we recommend using a center hold in place of a six o'clock hold or some other variation.

e. Trigger control is no more difficult nor any easier in International Rapid Fire than in 3-gun NRA shooting. It makes no difference what type of trigger we have on the gun, light or heavy, smooth or crisp, we must press the trigger smoothly and firmly straight to the rear parallel with the axis of the gun bore. Good NRA trigger control can be transferred to International Rapid Fire with only a speed-up to make it effective.

f. Grip is more critical in Rapid Fire than in the type of shooting we are accustomed to. Our grip must do two things. First it must allow us a natural sight alignment and second it must allow us to control the trigger in such a way that we can fire without disturbing the sight alignment. The use of orthopedic grips is authorized so long as they do not extend past the wrist joint. It is permissable to have the back of the hand covered. In fact a perfect fitting wooden glove would be an ideal grip for the rapid fire gun. To determine just what we need in an orthopedic grip, we use the same method as we use for making a custom grip on a "3-gun" hand-gun. Build up, take off, add on, until we finally get a grip that fits us exactly and have it duplicated. Requirements of the grip by the shooting hand is determined in the same manner we discussed in pistol Fundamentals I. Be sure to grip the pistol with enough tension to cause a tremor, then relax the tension slightly until the tremor stops. This should allow us to exercise independent control of the trigger and keep the sights in natural alignment.

g. There is no substitute for applying the fundamentals. That is the only way to be sure of getting a good shot. In International Rapid Fire, you can not leave anything to chance, nothing just happens of its own accord. It must be thought out, rehearsed and finally accomplished. Now you must employ your stance, position, grip breath control, sight alignment, and trigger control. You must plan exactly what you are going to do and have the intestinal fortitude to carry out your plan of action over all difficulties, actual or otherwise.

6. <u>Movement of Gun to the First Target:</u> Movement to the first and then subsequent targets is quite different from any shooting we have been accustomed to. Movement of gun to target has already been discussed to a point in both position and sight alignment. To delve deeper into the subject, how do we get this movement started and then, how do we get it stopped? The main point to remember in delivering the first shot: It must be fired in the center of the target with the sights aligned. This can only be done by having a smooth, well co-ordinated movement from "Ready" to "Fire" position. If any one shot can be given more value, it will have to be the first shot. If this shot is delivered properly, we set the pace for the remainder of the series. If we do something wrong on the first shot it tends to carry over to the remaining shots. For new and old International Rapid Fire shooters alike, first shot exercises are very beneficial to the training program.

a. Since we know that the "Ready Position" is with the shooting arm lowered 45°, what else must we know and do?

(1) First, the wrist and elbow must be locked, the tricep must be tensed. This aids us in controlling the movement to the first target and aids in reducing the arc of movement of the gun during our five shot series.

(2) Now we come to the problem of actually moving the arm to the firing position. This movement can be fast or slow depending upon the shooter and his state of training.

(a) Let us discuss first the fast movement to the target. We have here the apparent advantage of getting the sights to the center of the first target quickly, allowing us to fire the first shot sooner than we would if we brought the arm up slower. What actually happens here is the arm invariably over-shoots the aiming area and the time is wasted settling back into the center of the 10-ring. This over-shooting and settling negates any advantage gained by the fast movement. This fast movement is not recommended for new shooters, but is a definite advantage for a shooter who is skilled in International Rapid Fire and can overcome the disadvantages of this quick movement.

(b) The movement from "Ready" to "Fire" recommended for beginning shooters and also used by many good International Rapid Fire shooters is the so called "Slow" movement. Bear in mind that when we say "slow" we still mean that the shot must be delivered in no less than 1.25 to 1.50 seconds. In the slow movement the arm starts stopping almost as soon as it starts the movement This allows us to pick up our sight alignment in the lower part of the ten-ring, stop in the center, squeeze the trigger, almost all in one motion without having to hunt for the sights, settle down, or otherwise waste time delivering the first shot.

7. Movement of the gun to subsequent targets will be difficult for most of the experienced NRA type shooters. This, more than movement to the first target is different than anything we have been accustomed to. As we discussed in movement to the first target and firing, we must do everything correctly to aid us in firing the remainder of the series.

a. As the first shot fires, our recovery should take us to the center of the next target.

b. Stop, align the sights, press the trigger, recover on the next target and so on until we have fired the entire series.

c. No matter what you may hear, no successful shooter goes across the targets, firing without stopping. It is impossible to fire a good score this way. On each target, you must stop the arm and gun, align the sights and press the trigger.

8. Mental Discipline is applying all the mental processes toward a chosen goal. Mental discipline is essential in any thing we do which requires any degree of concentration. In International Rapid Fire, we need to be more mentally disciplined than in perhaps any other phase of shooting. The effort required to fire a series of shots is perhaps 95% mental effort and 5% physical effort. Therefore we can see why mental discipline plays such a large part in this type of shooting. As in any other field of endeavor, you can practice mental discipline anytime, anywhere. A good way to practice is to set up your chair or if possible your equipment at one end of the range. Dry fire with the competitors. If you can not dry fire, picture in your mind the sequence of events leading up to firing the first shot, set up in your mind how this shot will be fired, then mentally fire it, move to the next target, etc., until the series is completed. Actually, we cannot think about applying each of these fundamentals as they are employed. Rather, we must be trained and disciplined so that when each mechanical element falls into place, the employment of the fundamental will be automatic. For example, the mechanical movement of the target causes the mental impulse to start the movement of the arm to the aiming area. This mechanical movement of the arm causes the mental awareness of sight alignment. When the mechanical movement of the arm and attainment sight alignment is accomplished, the mental effort of trigger control takes place. The mechanical movement of the trigger finger results in the firing of the weapon. This in turn causes the mechanical movement to the next target and the mechanical/mental process starts all over again. This is nothing more than conditioning the body to react in a given way to a given set of conditions. When we have trained ourselves to the point where we will react properly when the targets turn, we are well on our way to becoming a good shooter.

These mental conditions can be set up only through intense effort and a good training program. When mastering International Rapid Fire, it is desirable to master one phase at a time. When this phase is mastered, move on to the next, still practicing what has been mastered. The reason for this approach is to insure the shooter learns the correct method and maintains his self-confidence.

FIGURE 12-1. THE RAPID FIRE PISTOL

FIGURE 12-2. SHOOTING THE RAPID FIRE PISTOL (SIDE VIEW)

92

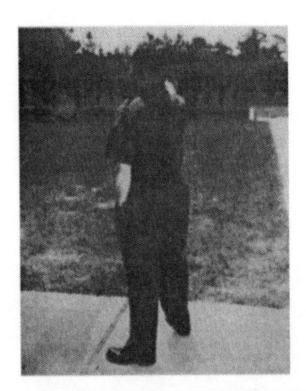

FIGURE 12-3. SHOOTING THE RAPID FIRE PISTOL (REAR VIEW)

FIGURE 12-4. THE STARTING POSITION

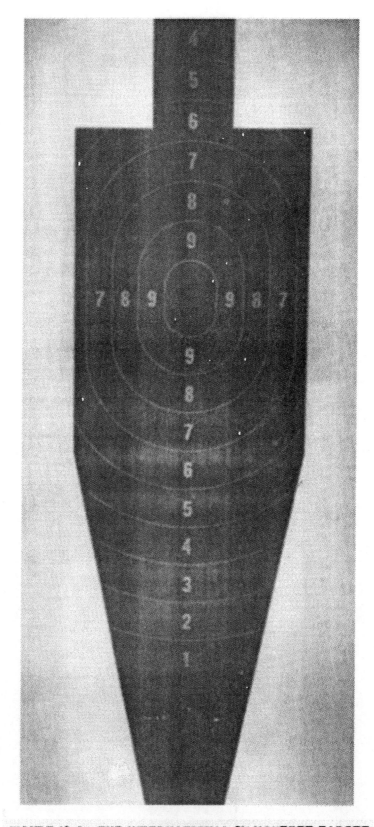

FIGURE 12-5. THE INTERNATIONAL SILHOUETTE TARGET

CHAPTER XIII

INTERNATIONAL CENTER FIRE

1. The ISU Center Fire 25 Meter Competition is fired generally with the .38 caliber pistol used in the NRA center fire event. However, any type of automatic pistol or revolver may be used, as long as the following stipulations are fulfilled:

    a. The calibre, as measured between the lands, shall be at least 7.62 mms and must not exceed 9.65 mms.

    b. The length of the barrel must not exceed 15 cms.

    c. The distance between the front sight and the rear sight must not exceed 22 cms.

    d. The sights must not be fitted with micrometer screws.

    e. The pull necessary to operate the trigger at the moment of discharge must not be less than (1.36 kgs), 3 lbs, measured vertically with vertical barrel.

    f. If a special grip is used, its width (at a right angle to the barrel) must not exceed 5 cms.

    g. The competitor must use the same type of gun (either pistol or revolver) and the same calibre in both the precision course and the rapid fire course.

    h. The calibers 7.6 - 9.65 mms include all British and American pistols and revolvers with nominal calibers 30, 32, 320, 32-20, 35, 357, 38 and 380.

    i. All sights of standard factory models are permitted as long as the adjusting screws can only be operated by means of a screwdriver or similar tool. Sights fitted with adjusting screws that can be operated by hand to effect adjustment for elevation and windage are prohibited.

2. The Center Fire International Course involves the firing of 30 rounds precision slow fire and 30 rounds rapid fire (silhouette) for a total of 600 points.

    a. Five rounds are loaded on command.

    b. Shooter fires at the 50 meter slow fire international target which is positioned at 25 meters. He has eight minutes to accomplish his zero string.

    c. After repairing targets, the shooter fires five rounds in six minutes at the repaired target. This is done six times for a total of 300 points. This completes the precision stage of fire.

    d. For the rapid fire stage the International Rapid Fire silhouette target is placed 25 yards distance with its edge facing the shooter.

    e. The shooter loads five rounds and faces the target with the shooting arm lowered to a 45° angle.

    f. The target is edged at the command "THE LINE IS READY." Ten seconds later the target is exposed in the faced position for three seconds, during which the shooter fires. The target edges after three seconds and reappears seven seconds later to be exposed another three seconds. This sequence is repeated until the target face has been exposed to the shooter five times.

NOTE: REMEMBER THAT THE TARGET REMAINS EDGED FOR TEN SECONDS ONLY AFTER THE INITIAL EDGING FOLLOWING THE COMMAND "THE LINE IS READY." ALL SUBSEQUENT EDGINGS OF THE TARGETS ARE SEVEN SECONDS IN DURATION. THE TARGETS ARE ALWAYS EXPOSED FOR A THREE SECOND INTERVAL.

3. The following steps represent an acceptable and effective method of accomplishing a high score in the precision stage of the International Center Fire Course.

    a. Obtain a firm proper grip on the weapon.

    b. Obtain an advantageous stance and position keeping in mind the added strain through training. This method is recommended since it tends to prevent the shooter from varying his grip as he raises the pistol. Variations in the grip will hinder the shooter's ability to maintain sight alignment because the variations in grip cause the front sight to be in different location in the rear sight notch each time his arm is raised to fire the next shot.

    c. As previously explained, the target will face the shooter after the initial ten second delay. The shooter must be totally committed to the task of anticipating the appearance of the target. The acquisition of a "pace" or "rhythm" also is essential here. Through constant observation and an attempt to be aware of the passage of time up are able to build a readiness. We in effect create a reflex response to the appearance of the target. From the moment the target edges or turns away we begin to build this readiness to respond to the suddenly reappearing target. As the seven seconds of target edge time passes, our readiness to respond to the facing action of the target builds to the point that our whole focus of attention is keyed to the first movement of the target as it begins to move into the faced position.

        (1) This total committment to one task is not easily attained. It requires concentration that must be developed through repeated attempts to accomplish this task of building a systematic readiness to respond as the seven seconds of edge time ticks away

        (2) One of the better rapid fire competitors describes his readiness to respond this way. "As I stand with my shooting arm at the prescribed 45° angle downward, I think of my arm as a tensed spring. One set of muscles wants it to spring into the pointing position but I prevent it from doing so with another set of muscles. When the target appears I release those detaining muscles and allow the set of muscles that will bring the arm up, to have their way."

        (3) However we describe it, we must be totally ready for the appearance of the target and respond in a split second!

    d. Not only must we raise the pistol as we described, but we must fire at the target. We have taken up any slack in the trigger while still pointed at the ground. The instant the target moves we begin the movement of the gun arm and hand towards it.

    e. During the time that the target is edged we look at it. We do not try to define the edge of the target too well. We do not gaze at it with a fixed focus.

    f. As the gun moves upward and the muzzle comes through the "hip" area on the target, we pick up our sights, try to align them, begin to press on the trigger and stop the gun hand in the center mass of the target.

        (1) Keep in mind that when the muzzle arcs through the hip area of the target we shift the eye from the target to the sights and from that time on through the firing of the shot our task is similar to that encountered in slow fire.

        (2) We focus on the sights, align them and keep moving the trigger to the rear until the shot breaks. In this course of fire we must attempt to keep the area of movement small, but we must continue to press positive on the trigger while we align the sights and try to stop all movement. We must fire the shot during the three seconds that the target will face us.

    g. There is a tendency to decrease pressure on the trigger or stop its rearward movement when the sights are badly misaligned and the gun arm is moving into the center point on the target. We must train our muscles to continue the pressure on the trigger while aligning sights. The targets will have faced and edged away if we follow the tendency of pulling the trigger only when the sights are in perfect alignment. It must be emphasized that the actions of pulling the trigger, aligning sights and stopping the gun in the center of the target are done in concert with one another. A smooth coordinated effort combining these three factors will cause the hammer to fall within the relatively short three second interval during which time the target is visible.

h. Most competitors try to breath normally during the first five seconds of the period of seven seconds of edged time. Approximately two seconds before the target is to face us, we stop breathing and await the appearance of the target.

(1) After the shot has been fired, we move the arm deliberately downward to the 45° angle and exhale the breath.

(2) We then breath normally and begin anew the process of increasing readiness during the time the target is edged. This culminates in total readiness and immediate response to the re-appearance of the faced target.

i. Endurance plays a vital role in shooting effective rapid fire. Early in our training we find that after the second or third shot, the muscles of the forearm begin to burn and ache. This feeling of discomfort must be borne without relaxating the grip, if possible. However, it may be necessary to relax the grip just slightly between shots during the early stages of training.

(1) Any exercise which will strengthen the arm is considered advantageous.

(2) Exercises which duplicate the action of raising and lowering the pistol would be the most desirable.

(3) Dry firing this event accomplishes the strengthening of the arm plus familiarizing us with the quick alignment of sights and movement of the trigger rearward.

FIGURE 13-1. THE CENTER FIRE PISTOL

FIGURE 13-2. SHOOTING THE CENTER FIRE PISTOL (SIDE VIEW)

FIGURE 13-3. SHOOTING THE CENTERFIRE PISTOL (REAR VIEW)

FIGURE 13-4. STARTING POSITION

FIGURE 13-5. THE PRECISION TARGET (INT'L 50 METER)

FIGURE 13-6. THE RAPID FIRE TARGET (INT'L SILHOUETTE)

CHAPTER XIV

INTERNATIONAL STANDARD PISTOL

The International Standard Pistol event is new to International Pistol Competition, dating from 1 January 1968. The fundamentals of Pistol shooting and the control techniques employed in the other International Pistol events are applicable to firing the Standard Pistol.

1. <u>DESCRIPTION OF PISTOL</u>: Any type of automatic pistol or revolver may be used, as long as the following stipulations are fulfilled:

    a. Ammunition: .22 Calibre Long Rifle only.

    b. The length of the barrel must not exceed 15 cms.

    c. The distance between the front sight and the rear sight must not exceed 22 cms.

    d. The sights must not be fitted with micrometer screws.

    e. The pull necessary to operate the trigger at the moment of discharge must not be less than 100 grams, measured vertically with vertical barrel.

    f. If a special grip is used, its width (at a right angle to the barrel) must not exceed 5 cms.

2. <u>The competitor must use the same type of gun (either pistol or revolver) and the same calibre in both the precision course and the rapid fire course.</u>

3. <u>COURSE OF FIRE</u>:

    a. Distance, 25 meters.

    b. Target, Free Pistol 50 meter International Slow Fire.

    c. Number of shots, 60.

    d. Stages of fire:

        20 shots, 4 series of 5 shots in 150 seconds (2 1/2min

        20 shots, 4 series of 5 shots in 20 seconds.

        20 shots, 4 series of 5 shots in 10 seconds.

        Sighting shots, 1 series of 5 shots in maximum of 150 seconds.

4. The standard pistol event is obligatory at World Championships.

5. For the total result of 60 shots, one medal will be awarded the individual winner, one medal the winning team.

FIGURE 14-1. THE STANDARD PISTOL

FIGURE 14-2. SHOOTING THE STANDARD PISTOL (SIDE VIEW)

FIGURE 14-3. SHOOTING THE STANDARD PISTOL (REAR VIEW)

FIGURE 14-4. STARTING POSITION

FIGURE 14-5. THE STANDARD PISTOL TARGET (INT'L 50 METER)

SECTION FIVE

SUPPLEMENTAL INFORMATION

ANNEX I

CHARACTERISTICS OF THE HUMAN BODY
RELEVANT TO STANCE, POSITION AND GRIP

The human motor apparatus is subdivided into two parts: active and passive.

The passive apparatus includes the bones and ligaments, both of which exert resistence as a result of their physical properties. The active apparatus includes the system of muscles which, by their relaxation and contraction, move individual portions of the body into different positions relative to one another, or which keeps them in a fixed position. A considerable part of this muscular action is involved in the maintenance of equilibrium or body balance.

A. PASSIVE APPARATUS.

1. The bones and their joints constitute the firm basis of the human body which is called the skeleton. The skeleton serves as the support for the soft tissues, particularly for the muscles attached to it.

Since the majority of bones have movable joints, they are able to change their position with respect to one another. The muscles attached to the bones, by contracting, keep individual portions of the skeleton steady, or conversely, put them in motion. Thus, the system of bones and muscles provides for various positions of the body in space, as well as for all kinds of movements which a person has to make constantly.

collar bone
shoulder joint
shoulder blade
sternum
ribs
shoulder bone
elbow joint
spinal column
ulno
radius
pelvis
hip bone

sacrum
coccyx
phalanges

thigh-bone

knee-cap
knee joint

tibia

femur

ankle joint
metatarsal bones

Figure 1-9. General View of the Human Skeleton.

a. The human body contains more than 200 bones which are joined to one another in various ways. The basis of the skeleton is the spinal column, consisting of individual vertebrae. The human spinal column has curves at the chest, small of the back, and sacrum (pectoral, lumbar, and sacral curves, respectively), which make it resilient and supple.

b. Two flat bones -- the shoulder blades -- are situated in the upper portion of the spine. They are attached to the spinal column and to the ribs only by means of muscles. Each shoulder blade is joined to the collar bone, or clavicle, the other end of which is joined to the breastbone, or sternum. The shoulder blades and collar-bones, encircling the upper portion of the torso, from the zone of upper extremities, or the shoulder, or humeral, zone.

c. The zone of the lower extremeties is the pelvic zone, or the pelvis. It consists of the sacrum and the two pelvic bones which are joined immobiley to it. The pelvic bones have round sockets into which fit the ends of the thigh bones (femur).

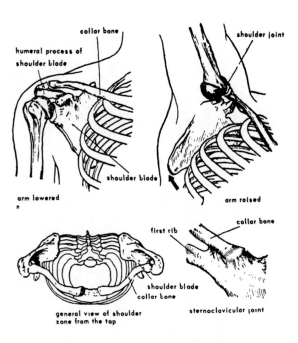

collar bone
humeral process of shoulder blade
shoulder blade
arm lowered
n

shoulder joint
arm raised

first rib
shoulder blade
collar bone
general view of shoulder zone from the top

collar bone
sternoclavicular joint

Figure 1-10. Bones of the Shoulder Zone.

d. The junctures between the bones are either immobile, of relatively low mobility, or mobile (joints). The majority of bones are joined mobilely to one another.

(1) The low mobility of some bone junctures is achieved by the layers of resilient cartilage between them. Such layers of cartilage are found, for example, between the individual vertebrae. When the muscles contract, these layers of cartilage squeeze together and the vertebrae almost touch one another (Figure 1-11).

Vertebrae

Cartilaginous layers

(2) Thus, the vertebrae, especially in the lumbar and neck areas, can be rather sharply inclined, relative to one another. As a whole, the entire spinal column will tolerate considerable movement, and will allow bending well forward, back, and to the sides. In addition to this suppleness, the spinal column has great durability, especially when functioning under the pressure of added weight. Considering the peculiarity of the skeletal structure, and the fact that the humeral zone is connected to the thorax and the spinal column principally by means of muscles, it becomes obvious that when shooting from a standing position, the shooter finds it difficult to support the weight of the pistol (up to 3 pounds suspended at the end of the arm) solely by means of these same muscles of the humeral (shoulder) zone. Consequently, the shooter must strive to give his body a stance which enables him to transfer some of the weight of the extended pistol arm onto the spinal column. In so doing, the shooter provides for a far greater percentage of bone support than is possible with a stance that relies solely on muscular tension.

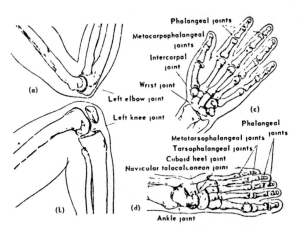

Figure 1-12. Movable Bone Junctures -- Joints: a. Left Elbow Joint; b. Left Knee Joint; c. Left Hand Joints; d. Left Foot Joints.

The most mobile bone junctures are the joints. The pouch of the joint consists of very compact connective tissue. In and around the layer of the pouch are strong, resilient tendinous ligaments. The edges of the pouch, together with the ligaments, are attached to the bones at a slight distance from their contiguous surfaces and form a tight seal over this joint cavity.

The movements are not identical in the various joints. Some joints permit movements only in two planes which are perpendicular to one another (bending and unbending as well as turning to the side, for instance). Still others provide for movement in any direction (bending and unbending, turning to the side, and rotation). The extent and direction of movement depend upon the form of the joint's surfaces.

Figure 1-13. Diagram Showing Placement of Ligament Apparatus: a. Hip Joint; b. Left Hand (Palm Surface); c. Right Foot (View From the Inside)

108

B. ACTIVE APPARATUS.

The active apparatus is composed of the muscular skeletal system, involuntary or smooth muscular system and the cardiac muscles.

The maintenance of equilibrium and the correct stance or posture of the body demands a very complicated, coordinated control system to govern the action of the entire skeletal musculature.

1. Skeletal muscular system. Let us now dwell briefly on the structure and properties of the skeletal muscles. Muscles having their ends attached to the bones of the skeleton are called skeletal muscles.

The entire skeletal musculature which keeps the human body in various positions and puts it in motion is composed of more than 600 muscles.

Muscluar tissue is distinguished by its ability to contract, that is, to change its form by shortening itself in length and by increasing in width.

A distinction is made between smooth, cardiac, and cross-striped muscular tissue.

a. Cross-striped muscles. (Voluntary)

The entire skeletal musculature is formed of cross-striped muscular tissue, the fibers of which consist of evenly alternating areas, some of which appear light-colored under the microscope, and the others of which appear dark, as a result of which the entire fiber appears to have transverse stripes. The contraction of the muscles is achieved by the shortening of the dark areas of its fibers.

End of nerve fiber

Sector of muscular fiber in state of contraction

Figure 1-14. Fibers of Cross-Striped Muscle.

As a result of the contraction of the muscles, the places where the muscles begin and are fastened to other parts of the skeleton are brought closer together and this results either in the movement of the body and the extremities or the maintaining of them in a definite position.

(1) The skeletal muscles are covered by a thin, resilient covering called the muscle fascia. At the ends of the muscle it changes into extremely tough white cords, the tendons. Frequently both ends of the muscle are fastened to two adjacent bones which are joined mobilely to one another; sometimes the tendons stretch very far, going past two or several joints. In portions of the arm there are many other such muscles. When they contract, to carry out their work, they can exert a certain overall movement not only upon the hand, but also upon the forearm, and, in its turn, this can have an adverse effect upon shooting. It must be said that the possibility of the isolated movement of one muscle without the participation of neighboring muscles depends in many instances upon training. It is possible, by means of training, to develop the ability to contract only those muscles which must carry out the particular movement and to weaken the effect of other muscles hindering the carrying out of that movement. It is extremely important for a shooter to achieve so-called isolated muscular contraction so that he will be able, for example, while shooting, to isolate that group of muscles in the arm which exerts the pressure on the trigger without at the same time changing the overall position assumed by the hand, that is, without putting it in motion.

(2) The work done by the muscle when it contracts can be of either of two types: static or dynamic.

(a) Static work of the muscles is carried out when the joints are in a certain position. During static work the muscles are capable of remaining in a strained position for only a relatively short period of time without fatigue.

(b) Dynamic work of the muscles is carried out when the individual portions of the body are to be moved; during such work, muscular tension alternates with relaxation, and contraction alternates with elongation.

b. During the period when the muscle is at work, a decomposition of certain substances which are part of the muscular fibers occurs in the muscle and lactic acid is formed. During the intervals between individual contractions, the muscle momentarily rests. This relaxation contributes to the restoration of the state which has existed prior to the contraction, and the muscle proves to be completely capable of operating again. However, if any muscle is in the contracted state continuously, fatigue develops rapidly; protracted contraction of a muscle can soon reduce it to the state of complete debility.

Figure 1-15. Muscles of Forward Surface of the Left Forearm and Hand.

c. When assuming the firing stance, at which time the shooter must achieve the greatest immobility of his body, the muscles perform static work. That is that work which is least favorable from the point of view of muscles fatigue. Taking this into consideration, the shooter must, especially when shooting for long periods of time, devote a great deal of attention to devising a system that allows alternating breaks between periods of assuming the firing position. This will make it possible for the muscles to regain their working ability to the greatest possible extent.

d. Muscles with identical action are called synergists. Muscles with opposing action are

e. It must be noted that the performing of smooth movements is possible only when antagonist muscles operate in concord. When they are in operation, the muscles of one group perform the action of a surmounting nature, and those of another group perform the action of a yielding nature. Without the participation of antagonist muscles, some synergist muscles would be able to carry out only jerky movements. The performing of physical exercises and training contribute not only to a situation in which the muscles become thicker, but also more elastic.

2. <u>Smooth muscles:</u> (Involuntary) The smooth muscles are encountered chiefly within the walls of the internal organs and are subject to comparatively weak excitability. These muscles have no bearing on assuming or maintaining a stance or posture.

3. <u>Cardiac muscles:</u> (Combination) The human heart is composed of muscles that are a combination of both voluntary and involuntary types. It is constructed of smooth (involuntary) muscle tissue but acts as the cross-striped or voluntary type muscle.

C. EQUILIBRIUM.

1. <u>Two basic types of equilibrium are involved in the balancing</u> of the human body, stable and unstable. These two types are determined by the location of the body's center of gravity relative to the support area.

a. Stable equilibrium is that in which the body, brought out of position of equilibrium and then left to itself, returns to the original position. This type of equilibrium occurs in instances when the body's center of gravity is located below the support area, for example, in the form shown in Figure 1-16.

b. Unstable equilibrium is that in which the body's center of gravity is located above the support area (Figure 1-17). In this instance the body which has been brought out of the state of equilibrium does not return to its orginal position.

Conseqnently, a person's body in position for shooting is in a state of unstable equilibrium, since the body's center of gravity is located above the support area.

2. <u>The principal condition for preserving any type of body equilibrium is that the line of gravity</u> (the vertical line dropped from the body's center of gravity) <u>must run through the support area.</u> If the line of gravity goes beyond the confines of the support area, a body which was in a state of unstable equilibrium will not return to the original position, but will fall.

Being in a state of unstable equilibrium, the body can have a varying degree of stability, depending upon the position in which it is located, since the degree of the body's stability is determined by the height of its center of gravity above the support area, the size of the support area itself, and by the presence of the line of the center of gravity within the borders of the support area.

a. Since equilibrium is upset at the moment when the body's line of gravity goes beyond the limits of the support area (Figure 1-17), it is completely obvious that when the support area is unchanged, the body will lose its stability in proportion to the height of the center of gravity above the support area. With an increase in support area, the body's stability increases when the height of the center of gravity remains unchanged. Another essential factor determining the degree of the body's stability is the position of the line of gravity with respect to the borders of the support area. The closer the body's line of gravity approaches the edge of the support area, the fewer the possibilities of shifting it in that direction without risking the chance of upsetting the body's equilibrium. The least stable position is standing. The small degree of stability of this position is caused by the fact that, with a small support area, the body's center of gravity is located comparatively high above it. With identical height of the center of gravity and identical support area, the standing position will have varying degrees of stability depending upon how the shooter distributes the weight of his body. It depends on whether he inclines the body back, standing on his heels; or stands erect, placing his weight upon the middle portion of each foot and thus bringing the line of gravity closer to the center of the support area, or leans the body forward, placing the principal part of his weight on the front portion of the feet and forcing the line of gravity to approach the forward edge of the support area.

(a) Stable equilibrium   (b) Unstable equilibrium

Figure 1-16. Types of Equilibrium of the Human Body.

Figure 1-17. Unstable Equilibrium and Loss of equilibrium.

b. Thus, the location of the body's center of gravity above the support area, the size of the support area, and the location of the line of gravity with respect to the borders of the support area are the external factors which determine the degree of bodily stability.

(1) Let us examine first of all the question of the center of gravity of the human body. Since our body consists of separate parts, its over-all center of gravity is defined as the center of gravity of a system of bodies. Insofar as the separate parts of the human body are joined mobilely to one another, the over-all center of gravity does not have a fixed position, but shifts with every change in position of its separate parts. Therefore each posture or position of the parts of the body located in a state of equilibrium has, correspondingly, contributed to a different location of the body's over-all center of gravity (Figure 1-18).

The over-all center of gravity of the human body shifts slightly even when the body remains in one and the same posture. As a result of breathing, blood circulation, and the filling up of the organs in the abdominal cavity, it is very difficult to achieve absolute accuracy in determining the location of the over-all center of gravity of a living organism. As applicable to the separate postures of the body it can be said, for example, that when the body is in its ordinary symmetrical stance, the over-all center of gravity of a person's body is located at a point representing 0.555-0.565 of his height.

Properly speaking, in practice the shooter does not have to know or to determine accurately the location of the over-all center of gravity in his body, but by knowing about the influence which a shift in the center of gravity has upon the degree of stability of a particular stance, the shooter must strive only to achieve a posture in which the weight of the body is distributed evenly onto his support surfaces-both feet.

Figure 1-18. Location of Common Center of Gravity of the Human Body in Various Poses.

112

(2) The body's stability is dependent upon the size and shape of the support area. The support area is made up not only of the body's support surfaces--the feet--but is also the area lying between them. The shooter can, for example, when in a standing position, place his feet differently, decrease or increase the support area, and thus substantially change stability conditions of his body (Figure 1-19).

Figure 1-19. Change in the Body's Support Area Depending Upon the Placement of the Feet.

c. As a result, let us examine the structure of the foot, its operation, and the least favorable conditions for it. When a person's body is in a standing position, the foot muscles are carrying out the greatest amount of static work.

(1) The foot is an arched structure with inner, outer, and transverse arches (Figure 1-20). The arches are of importance distributing the weight of the body onto a large surface when the person is standing, and also for reducing the shocks occuring when a person moves.

(2) Taking into consideration the structure of the foot, and the location and development of its muscles, it can be noted that (the support points of the arches are: the protuberance of the heel-bone; and in the front, the large ends of the first and fifth metatarsal bones. These form the so-called support triangle (Figure 1-21).

Figure 1-20. Diagram of the Structure of the Foot.

Figure 1-21. Support Triangle of the Foot.

(3) Distinction is made between the complete surface and the "active" support surface of the foot. The former, which is visible in an impression of the foot, is larger than the "active" surface, since its soft portions do not take direct participation in supporting the weight of the body. If the person wears a boot, the "active" support surface increases considerably. It is fitting here to mention that the shooter must devote a considerable amount of attention to his footwear, making sure that the heels of his boots are not worn down, the soles are not warped, and that the toes are not turned up.

(4) The support area when standing with heels together is the largest when the feet are placed at a slight angle to one another. When the feet are spread apart, the largest support area is achieved by keeping them parallel to one another. However, the following must be kept in mind: from the point of view of the arch structure of the foot and the method of supporting the arches, it is extremely disadvantageous when standing to put the load on the inner arch. The internal arch contains more bones and consequently more joints, and, second, it is supported almost exclusively by muscles. Investigations have shown that with an increase in the angle between the toes of the shoes, or when the feet are spread to the sides, there is an increase in the load upon the inner arch.

Center of the Support Area

Figure 1-22. Most Convenient Placement of the Feet When Assuming Position for Firing.

Therefore, the pistol shooter, when preparing to fire must in no instance place his feet very far apart or place his feet at a wide angle relative to one another. As shown by practice, it is most advantageous, when preparing to fire from a standing position, to place the feet and to distribute the weight of the body over the support area as shown in Figure 1-22.

d. When considering the problem of the stability of the human body in a particular position, one must not limit oneself to the application of just the general laws of mechanics which determine in general the equilibrium of physical bodies. Under different conditions--identical support area, identical location of the over-all center of gravity, and one and the same line of gravity--a person's body can occupy completely different positions and can actually have varying degrees of stability (Figure 1-23). As can be seen from the drawing, the distinguishing feature of these two positions of the body is the fact that the preservation of their equilibrium is achieved by completely different work by the inner forces of the organism.

If certain muscles are relaxed, the equilibrium of various parts of the person's body is upset. Each part shifts downward toward its center of gravity and consequently the over-all center of gravity of the body also shifts. If the line of the center of gravity moves outside the limits of the support area, the body falls.

This peculiarity of the statics of the human body may be explained by the fact that equilibrium may be achieved and maintained only if certain muscular control functions are operating efficiently. When the muscular apparatus functions efficiently, the tension of the various muscles counteracts the weight of the separate parts of the body, and the bodily equilibrium is maintained with a minimum of effort.

The effects of gravity, and the counteraction on the part of the muscles, cannot create an absolute equilibrium of the body. As a result, the body moves to a greater or lesser extent.

The shooter is always confronted by the task of selecting a stance in which the balancing of the body requires the least expenditure of muscular effort. Under such conditions the body will be subject to the least back and forth swaying movement.

     e. Let us examine the state of the body's equilibrium in the standing position. In general the body may be held in such a position that a large number of the parts of the human body that are mobile with respect to one another, may be maintained in a fixed state by means of muscles and ligaments (Figure 1-24). The entire operation of the muscles during this process is of a static nature. The ligaments also play a substantial role in maintaining the body in a standing position.

Figure 1-23. Example of the Different Positions of the Body with Identical Support Area, an Almost Identical Location of the Over-all Center of Gravity, and with the Line of the Body's Center of Gravity Running Identically.

Figure 1-24. Equilibrium of the Various Parts of the Body When Standing.

     f. Let us now examine, in general outlines, the three basic types of standing positions: anthropometric ("normal posture"), rest ("comfortable posture"), and strained (military").

(1) In the anthropometric position where body weight is carried evenly distributed between toe and heel (Figure 1-25a), the vertical line of the center of gravity coincides with the transverse axes of the hip, knee, and ankle joints. In this instance the ligament apparatus plays a considerably lesser role in reinforcing the joints than the muscles do. In this position the parts of the body--the pelvis, hip, shin, and foot--are in a state of somewhat unstable equilibrium, and this leads to an inevitable, and rather considerable, rocking of these parts back and forth. The muscles reinforcing the joints thus prove to be strained alternately from the front and from the back. In the standing position, when the mobile parts of the body are kept rigid at the joints chiefly by means of the work of the muscles, the rocking is more perceptible than in other standing positions.

(2) In the rest position, slightly forward (Figure 1-25b), the vertical line of the center of gravity runs in back of the transverse axes of the hip joints and in front of the knee and ankle joints. The reinforcement of the position of the pelvis relative to the femur is contributed to by the muscles and ligaments. A special role is played by the iliofemoral ligament, which is so strong that, when it is tense, it can support the weight of the torso even without the participation of the muscles. The reinforcement of the knee joints is carried out by the ligaments and muscles located in back of those joints. The reinforcement of the knee joints is carried out by the ligaments and muscles located in back of those joints. The reinforcement of the ankle joints (with the shin inclined forward) contributes to the arrangement of the joints themselves, the lower end of the tibia (shin) and the ankle bone (astragalus).

Figure 1-25. Basic Types of Body Position Standing.

(3) In the strained position, too far forward (Figure 1-25c), the vertical line of the center of gravity runs in front of the transverse axes of the hip, knee, and ankle joints. Therefore, in order to prevent the body from falling, the muscles located on the back surfaces of those joints must constantly be in a greatly contracted state.

Comparing the work of the muscles in the different forms of standing positions, it can be said that the rest position corresponds to the specifications for the least expenditure of muscular effort on the part of the organism to preserve equilibrium. Consequently, the variation of the bodily standing position in which the vertical line of the center of gravity runs in back of the transverse axes of the hip joints and in front of the knee and ankle joints, that is, when the torso is bent slightly backward and the pelvis is moved imperceptibly forward, must be the basis for assuming a stance when firing. The shooter must inevitably come to this conclusion because the reinforcement of the basic joints of the body is achieved not so much by the work of the muscles as by the inclusion of the ligament apparatus into the work. This contributes to the mutual reinforcement of the mobile parts of the body in the joints and consequently to the acheivement of the best rigidity of the shooter's entire body, together with the least expenditure of muscular effort.

116

Such is the over-all, elementary, and far from complete information on human motor apparatus which the present-day shooter must have.   Otherwise, it will be very difficult, if not impossible, for him to find a stance which is correct and advantageous for him.

ANNEX II

OPTICAL PROPERTIES OF THE HUMAN EYE RELEVANT TO SIGHT ALIGNMENT

A. GENERAL

The principal difficulties which confront the shooter during aiming are determined by the inherent characteristics of the organ of vision--the eye-- and its work as an optical apparatus during the aiming process.

It is well known that the aiming process makes very exacting demands upon the vision, since consistency and degree of accuracy are directly dependent upon the sharpness of vision and the conditions determing them. Therefore, it is necessary for the shooter to have a knowledge of certain of the optical properties of the eye. He must know the degree and the conditions under which the optical imperfections of the eye can affect the accuracy of aiming.

Figure 2-5. Horizontal Cross Section of the Human Eye (Right Eye)

1.   Cornea (transparent, glasslike portion of coat of eyeball.)
2.   Conjunctiva (mucous membrance which lines eyelids and is reflected onto eyeball.)
3.   Ciliary muscle (smooth muscles, controlling alteration of crystalline lens)
4.   Muscle of eyeball
5.   Space posterior to crystalline lens
6.   Sclera (toughest of the three membranes, forming the outer protective and supporting layer of the eyeball)
7.   Choroid (vascular coat of the eye)
8.   Retina (innermost tunic of the eye, containing receptors, rods and cones)
9.   Optic disk (blind spot of retina)
10. Optic nerve (transfers images from retina to visual nerve centers located in the brain)
11. Anterior chamber (filled with aqueous humor)
12. Iris (opening in center is called the pupil, contains groups of smooth muscles that dilate and contract pupil)
13. Posterior chamber (filled with aqueous humor)
14. Suspensory ligaments (zonule of Zinn)
15. Crystalline lens (transparent biconvex body enclosed in transparent sheath, suspended from ciliary body by suspensory ligaments)
16. Vitreous (transparent jelly-like substance contained within transparent membrane close to retina)
17. Fovea central is (a pit in the middle of the macula lutea)
18. Macula Lutea (point of clearest vision, contains greatest number of cones)

B. OPTICAL PROPERTIES OF THE HUMAN EYE.

The human eye as a visual analyzer makes it possible to distinguish rather accurately between colors, form, dimensions, degree of illumination, and the location of objects in the immediate environment (Figure 2-5).

1. <u>The forward portion of the eye,</u> which is turned toward the light, contains a light-refracting apparatus which transmits the image to a light-sensitive membrane--the retina; this apparatus consists of a system of refracting media and surfaces--the cornea, the crystalline lens, the aqueous humor, and the vitreous humor filling the optical cavity. (The light-refracting apparatus also includes the ciliar humor and the iris, which has an opening, the pupil, in the center of it.)

2. <u>The degree of illumination,</u> the form and location of the objects surrounding us are perceived by the internal light-sensitive membrane--the retina--which is linked by means of the optic nerve to the cerebral cortex. In order to obtain the correct visual perception of any object, the image of it upon the retina must be sharp. This is achieved as a result of the eye's ability to adapt its light-refracting system and thus to obtain on the retina a sharp image of objects located at varying distances from it.

3. <u>In our eye, the role of photographic lens is played by the crystalline lens</u> which is a transparent, biconvex body similar in form to an ordinary lens. When the eye observes objects located at varying distances, the curvature of the crystalline lens changes, as a result of which the eye's optical system adapts by reflex and very rapidly to the perceiving of objects located at varying distances from us. As a result, the image produced on the retina is a sharp one and this makes it possible to perceive correctly and sharply the form and outlines of the objects surrounding us. This ability of the eye to adapt to the viewing of various objects located at varying distances from the eye by means of changing the curvature of the crystalline lens (changing the refraction) is called accomodation.

4. <u>Consequently, the human eye is constructed in such a way that it is not able to see sharply,</u> simultaneously, objects located at varying distances from it. Therefore, it is not possible when aiming, to see with identical sharpness the sight alignment and the target which is located at varying distances from the shooter's eye. Understanding this, one must not strain the vision excessively in vain attempts to see everything sharply at the same time.

5. <u>The normal eye in the state of rest</u> is set up to perceive distant objects, that is, it is set to infinity. In order to switch the vision to perceive objects located close by, it is necessary to exert a definite muscular effort. The mechanism of accomodation lies in the fact that the ciliary muscle contracts, and the crystalline lens takes on a convex form, thus increasing its refraction.

As a result, when aiming, one must not abuse the eye by shifting the glance with excessive frequency, from one point of clear vision to another. For example, a shift of focus from the rear notch and the front sight to the target, and back again. The protracted muscular effort expended under such conditions leads to the rapid and considerable fatiguing of the oculo-motor muscles. For the same reason, the shooter must not aim for long sustained periods. He must make sure that in the intervals between sequences of aiming, he does not concentrate his glance on some object, but looks momentarily into the distance "with an absent-minded stare" in order to rest his eye muscles.

6. <u>When there is a change in the force of natural illumination,</u> the level of the eye's light-sensitivity changes and the eye adapts to the different amount of light entering it. A role similar to that played by the diaphragm in a camera is played by the pupil, the opening or aperture in the middle of the iris. Under the action of various eye muscles, the diameter of the pupil can be made narrower or wider. It is this action which regulates the amount of light entering the eye and which improves the depth of focusing of the image upon the retina when the pupil becomes narrower. The question of the speed at which the pupil reacts to a change in illumination is also deserving of attention. When the light changes to greater brilliance, the pupil contracts much more rapidly than it expands after finding itself again in conditions of lesser brilliance. For example, the contraction of the pupil to the stable level of average light intensity takes about 5 seconds, but the process of its reverse dilation after the stimulus created by low intensity light requires about 3 minutes. From this the shooter must also make the corresponding conclusions: in order to preserve the eye's working efficiency without reducing the accuracy of aiming, before or during aiming, one must not look at brightly illuminated objects or, moreover, subject

the eye to the action of sharp transitions from light to shadow. In the intervals between shots, one must not rest the eyes by closing them. Between shots, it is necessary to rest the eyes, but the best way is to look at distant dull surfaces having even tones of gray, green, or blue.

C. FUNCTION OF THE HABITS OF THE NORMAL EYE.

All shooters should make a conscious effort to improve the condition of their eyes in the intervals when they are not actually aiming by allowing the habits of normal sight of function. The following will give an idea of how this should be done. There are three things that every healthy eye does: Blink, center its attention (called Central Fixation) and shift.

1. <u>Blinking</u>, the first habit of normal sight an involuntary action. The blink is the quick, light, easy closing and opening of the eye, and it is done intermittently by every normal eye. The rate of blinking varies with people and also varies with the use an eye is put to. You blink more, for instance, when you look at something brilliant than you do when you look at something soft in tone.

a. Frequently the dividing point between a normal and abnormal pair of eyes is its impulse to blink under a given situation. If the eyes are perfectly normal, they will blink; suppression of the act of blinking shows a tendency to become abnormal.

b. The action of the eyelids in blinking is most essential to normal eyes and sight. The fluid that keeps the eyes moist is produced by a small gland called the lacrimal gland under the outer portion of the upper lid. When one blinks, this fluid is washed down and over the eyeball and keeps the eye moist.

This moisture has several functions:

(1) There is a definite antiseptic and cleansing action of the fluid.

(2) The brilliance of the eyes and their ability to reflect light are largely due to the fluid on their surface.

(3) The fluid is essential to the cornea, which is the small translucent front part of the eye. Since the cornea has no blood vessels, it needs this fluid to keep it moist or it may develope corneal ulcers.

(4) When particles of foreign matter get into the eye, the lacrimal fluid tends to float them off, while on an eye that is dry, the particles may stick and imbed themselves.

(5) In cold weather, frequent blinking tends to keep the eye warm. An eyeball can be very uncomfortable when cold.

(6) In strong wind or when the weather is very dry, blinking comforts and protects the eye. Under these conditions, one should blink frequently, almost continuously, because the fluid is lost so rapidly.

(7) In the short interval of blinking, the muscles of the pupil have a chance momentarily to relax their tension.

(8) Blinking also enables the eye to move slightly and thus allows the recti muscles to make the small amount of movement essential to their well-being, since motion is necessary to the health of any muscle.

(9) The circulation of the lymphatic fluid around the eye is aided by blinking, and the eye is strengthened by this good circulation, just as any body is benefited by keeping the circulation of the blood active around it.

c. Blinking is not an interruption of continuous vision. Continuous vision is the illusion that a normal eye produces, authentic in effect but nevertheless an illusion. When an image falls on the retina, there is another image or an after-image produced. In other words, the image remains on the retina for a short period longer than the image is kept before the eye. It is as if your image in the mirror, stayed there a moment after you had gone away.

120

Thus, it is not necessary for the eye to be seeing actively all the time in order to produce the illusion of seeing constantly. In fact, nothing in the body works more than half time or so much as half time. More than half of the time of every organ is consumed in the repair and replacement of its own tissue and the elimination of its waste products.

d. The frequency of the visual impressions made by the eye is between thirty and forty images per second in the average person. Therefore the blink does not interfere with constant vision. It is possible for the eye to blink so frequently that the eye is close on-half of the time and yet it will see as much as if it were open all the time.

e. In fact, blinking increases the actual amount of time you may actively see, since failing to blink constitutes strain and this may reduce the number of images from thirty or forty to twenty or fewer images per second. There is no single instance where blinking interferes with sight. It is a natural, constructive performance and improves the eye. If for some reason the eye has not been blinking normally, the resumption of normal blinking improves its vision.

f. Do not confuse a wink or a spasm of the eyelid with blinking. A spasm of the eye lid is a forceful, involuntary constriction of the lid and usually involves the muscles around the eye as well as the muscles of the eyelid and is frequently associated with some nervous disease. A blink is a light, easy, smooth, barely noticeable movement of the eyelid.

g. If you have formed a habit of looking too fixedly at things, remind yourself to blink. Blink consciously and often. Condition your reactions until you again have the unconscious blink.

2. Central fixation: The second habit of normal sight is to have the eye and the mind so coordinated that they fix on a small area at one and the same time. In other words, when you look at an object you should localize your attention, fasten it on the one small area, not scatter it.

a. For example, when you look at a page of print, you cannot see the whole page clearly. If you fix your eyes on the upper right-hand corner of the page, you can see that clearly, but the remainder of the page, although it is within your field of vision, is much less clear. To see the last word on the page clearly, you will have to shift your eyes so that they are directed straight at that word.

b. The same is true if you take words quite close to each other. To see the first word of a line clearly you must look directly at it, and to see the last word on that line it is necessary to shift the eye. The same is true if you want to see the second word on the line clearly. You can see it well enough to read it, but you do not see it perfectly clear when you are looking at the first word. A definite strain is involved if you try to see it that way. This is true down to the very smallest degree of space.

c. There is a basic, structural reason for this. The Macula Lutea, the only part of the eye that sees perfectly clear, is in the center of the retina and is no larger than the head of an ordinary steel pin. This dot of perfect sight is placed in the eye like a point at the bottom center of a bowl whose sides slope gently like an arena. This one tiny point has clear, strong vision. When your vision departs from that point, there is a tremendous reduction in clarity of sight. There is, instead, blurred, collateral vision. And this is increasingly blurred as you continue out from the center until near the outside edge there is only perception of general shape, color and motion.

d. Since only this point, the Macula Lutea, has perfectly clear vision, only a very small area can be seen clearly at one time. But the movement of shifting is so swift that the illusion of seeing a large area is given. The images falling on the Macula Lutea are carried swiftly into the visual brain centers, one succeeding another with such rapidity that there are thirty or forty and sometimes more images a second, thus creating the illusion of a whole picture in the brain.

e. This ability of the brain to carry successive images and so produce the illusion of clearly seeing the whole object or a considerable area is an impressive and beautiful fact, but it is also a cause of trouble to the shooter. One comes to believe that the eye itself can see a large area clearly, and so misuse slips in because any attempt to do this is to use the eye without focusing!

f. "Large Area" means trying to see for example, two words or more at a time. The healthy, normal eye habitually sees only a very small area at given moment. The mind and the eye normally coordinate perfectly on each word or point of observation with no effort or impulse to see more just as it does when one is writing.

If the practice of seeing a large area at one time persists over a sufficient length of time, the ability to focus perfectly is lost and the blurred vision naturally to the collateral area is the only vision possible. It is then necessary to retrain the eye and mind to look at only a small area in order to again have central fixation without which no vision can be clear and normal.

g. One can read indefinitely without undue tiring or harming the eyes in any way if the eyes are relaxed and the vision is localized. But, if the seeing power of the collateral field of vision is used, the eye is straining and there is a resulting fatigue and loss of efficiency.

The fact that the eye sees clearly only a very small area at any one time cannot be over-stressed. In the awareness of this fact rests the coordinating of the mind with the structural limitations of the eye, without which there cannot be normal vision.

If you grasp this fact of focused vision and mentally close your sight to a large area, you will attain this valuable habit of central fixation and find increased efficiency in the use of your eyes in shooting.

3. Shifting. The third beneficial habit of normal eyes is to shift. This seems to quarrel with the second habit which is to localize your gaze but in reality it does not. You must point your gaze, but you must, too, constantly shift your point of vision.

If you do not shift it, you will stare, and staring is one of the worst and commonest forms of eye strain.

a. Shifting is a normal function and is normally done unconsciously. The frequency with which your eyes shift varies with the type of demand upon the eyes; for instance, looking at a book or watching a tennis match. The book is stationary and the eyes do not tend to move, while the tennis balls and players are constantly in motion so the eyes must move continually in order to follow them.

b. But, in any event, shifting should be as frequent as possible. The time required for an image to register on the retina, about 1/50 of a second, allows for a great frequency of shifting with no loss or interruption of vision.

c. People who are inclined to look at one area too long, and every abnormal eye does this, would benefit both in vision and in eye comfort if frequent shifting from the point being looked at is con-sciously practiced. If your vision is abnormal; without wearing your glasses look at a word, then look at a word three word spaces beyond it; then back up to the original word. Do this until both words be-come clear. Be relaxed while you practice.

d. Or, if your vision is good; look at the moon and while blinking frequently, shift your vision from one point to another on the moon. Do this a number of times and the moon will stand out much more clearly and appear in its true form as a solid spherical body with depth and shape instead of a flat disc.

e. Shifting is both voluntary and involuntary in character. The involuntary shift is con-tinuous, automatic and very slight. This movement is not visible and is believed to correspond in fre-quency with the rate of image production in the retina.

f. There is in every muscle a faint tremor, since muscle tone is not a constant factor but is a rapid succession of contractions producing a relatively steady muscle pull. And, since the eyes are held in position by muscles and all focusing is produced by these muscles, the eyes are naturally subject to all conditions that muscles produce incidental to their normal functioning.

g. When the eye is relaxed, the voluntary shifting is frequent and the movement is short in scope. The tense eye can make a large movement, but it requires relaxation and normality for an eye to keep shifting in relaxed condition with a very small movement. This is true of all muscles--the finer the movement, the better trained and the more relaxed must be the muscle. When an eye is strained and the vision is abnormal, practice in shifting frequently will give relief from the strain and produce improvement in the vision.

h. An exercise that accomplishes this is to focus definitely on each word and consciously shift to the next one. A few minute's practice each day will make this an unconscious habit.

i. Normal shifting is absolutely essential to normal sight. Loss of vision is frequently in direct proportion to the loss of motion.

4. In addition to acquiring the three habits described above, a shooter may find it desirable to strengthen his tolerance for light. This may be done as described in the following paragraphs:

a. Sunlight is very beneficial to the eyes. It both relaxes and stimulates. But it is necessary to know how to use the sunshine to get the most out of it. Sunlight directly on the eyes may cause great damage. The eye can be strengthened in its light tolerance by judicious exposure to light. One of the most effective and simple ways of strengthening the eyes is to expose them to the sun's rays in the following manner:

(1) Close the eyes lightly as the face is turned directly toward the sun. Keeping the eyes closed, slowly turn the head from side to side. Keep this up for four or five minutes. Then, when the eyes are relaxed from the heat of the sun and the motion of the head, they may be opened, but only momentarily, and when the head is turned to the side. The eyes must not look directly at the sun but may look near it. Make no effort to see, and open the eyes only in flashes. As this exercise is continued, and the eyes become accustomed to the increased light, the glance may be directed closer and closer to the sun.

(2) By doing this with regularity on successive days and for a gradually increasing length of time, any eye will be strengthened and its vision improved.

b. The eye is admirably equipped to protect itself and function under widely varying light conditions. When the natural protective mechanism is used, as just outlined, strong light will be handled easily by the eye.

D. OPTICAL IMPERFECTIONS OF THE HUMAN EYE.

As a result of optical various imperfections of the eye, the images of objects on the retina have edges which are not completely sharp, or are to a degree totally fuzzy. As a consequence, there exists a certain limit of varying sensitivity of our eye which determines the sharpness of vision. It must be said that sharpeness of vision, in and of itself, is inconstant. It has a certain variable value which depends upon the degree and the conditions under which, the optical imperfections of the eye have a noticeable effect. Therefore, the shooter must know, at least in overall features, the conditions which influence the sharpness of vision and thus the degree of accuracy of aiming.

As an optical instrument, the eye has inherent in it, the phenomena of aberration and diffraction of light.

1. Spherical aberration is a function of the eye in which rays of light falling upon the crystalline lens are refracted differently and are not focused at a single point. The extreme outer rays are refracted more strongly than the central ones (Figure 2-6). As a result of spherical abberration, a beam of parallel rays entering the eye is focused on the retina not in the form of a sharp image, but in the form of a circle of light diffusion. The size of the circle of light diffusion resulting from spherical aberration is in direct proportion to the size of the pupillary opening. It is obvious that the sharpness of the image is increased if one eliminates extreme rays. Consequently, as the pupillary opening contracts, the sharpness of the image of the object upon the retina increases.

The degree to which spherical aberration can hinder the seeing of objects sharply, and to which the sharpness of the image depends upon the size of the pupillary opening, can be convincingly shown to the shooter by means of a simple example. Small orienting marks and objects which can be distinguished only with difficulty during overcast weather become incomparably more discernible if one looks at them through a small peep hole which, in this instance, fulfills the role of an artificial pupil.

Figure 2-6.   Phenomenon of Spherical Aberration.

2.   The phenomenon of light diffraction lies in the fact that light rays passing through small openings, particularly through the crystalline lens; seem to bend (figure 2-7) and produce on the retina an image not in the form of a single sharp point, but in the form of a circle surrounded by a number of concentric light rings of decreasing sharpness.   This occurs as a result of the wave nature of light.

a.   As the pupillary opening decreases, the diameter of the diffraction ring of light diffusion increases.   The diffraction rings around the images have a noticeably telling effect only when there are extremely small dimensions of the pupil, and this, as we can see, is a certain opposite of the phenomenon of spherical aberration.   The phenomenon of diffraction makes itself felt when there is solar illumination from the front and the sun in shining into the eyes; when there are bright patches of sunlight on the horizontal surfaces of the front and rear sights etc.

Figure 2-7.   Phenomenon of Diffraction of Light on the Pupil

b.   The operation of the eye as an optical apparatus is also harmed to a certain degree by the light diffusion occurring with in it.   It is especially discernible when one views brightly illuminated objects located against a dark background.   The effect of light diffusion in the form of a more or less noticeable radiation, covering the field of vision, is caused by media which do not possess absolute transparency--the crystalline lens and the vitreous humor.   The light diffusion in the optical media is responsible for the halos of light.   They are especially noticeable where the targets are strongly illuminated by sunlight.   In such an instance, the white background of the target casts a sharp reflection and causes a considerable light diffusion in the optical media.   This causes a blinding effect.   Both the bull's-eye, perceived by the eye in the form of a gray spot with indistinct edges, and the front and rear sights are perceived with unclear outlines.

c. It is obvious from what has been said that the amount of light diffusion from spherical aberration is in direct proportion to the size of the opening of the pupil, and the amount of light diffusion from diffraction is in inverse proportion to the size of the opening of the pupil, and thus it is not possible to eliminate these types of diffusion completely. As a result of this inverse dependence of the effects of aberration and diffraction upon the size of the pupil, the best conditions of sharp vision correspond to a certain average size of the pupillary opening--a diameter of approximately 3mm.

Taking this into consideration, depending upon the conditions of illumination which influence the size of the pupillary opening, the shooter must strive, insofar as he can, to create the most favorable conditions for the operation of the eye. He must protect his eyes from the action of light by using visors, filter type shooting glasses, or by possibly using an artificial pupil. An eye disc device is attached to the shooting glasses with adjustment for varying diameters. He must also make sure that the sights do not shine and thus produce a blinding effect upon the eye: They must be carefully and evenly blackened.

d. Brilliant sources of light harm the eye chiefly by means of the violet sector of the visible and invisible portions of the spectrum. The complete elimination of the violet sector of the spectrum is achieved by yellow, yellow-green, and yellow-orange light filters. Such light filters not only do not reduce the acuity of visibility, but, on the contrary, increase it. Type of darker glass protecting the eyes from brilliant sources of light somewhat reduce the acuity of vision. However, by having an assortment of shooting glasses of varying shades, it is possible to select and use them in such a way that the shooter's eye perceives the correct sight alignment under the brightest illumination in almost the same way that he does during overcast weather.

3. Nearsightedness, farsightedness and astigmatism: The optical imperfections of the eye also include nearsightedness, farsightedness, and astigmatism, the existence of which also hinders the correct focusing of the optical system of the eye and the obtaining of sharp images of objects upon the retina.

a. If the eye is constructed in such a way that rays of light entering it in a parallel beam are focused exactly on the retina without any effort at accommodation, we say that the eye is a normal one. (Figure 2-8a.)

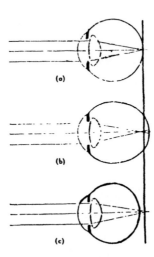

Figures 2-8. Schemes Showing the Refraction Rays in the Eyes: (a) Normal, (b) Nearsighted (c) Farsighted.

b. The eye is nearsighted if the rays entering it in a parallel beam are focused in front of the retina (Figure 2-8b). Nearsightedness is caused either by the fact that the eyeball is excessively long from front to back or by the fact that the eye has great refracting force, or by a combination of both factors. Nearsightedness can be corrected comparatively easily by means of eyeglasses. Many pistol shooters suffer from nearsightedness, but this defect of vision, after being corrected by the

125

proper choice of eyeglasses; does not prevent them from achieving record-making competitive results.

c. The eye is farsighted if the rays entering it are focused in back of the retina (Figure 2-8c). This can occur either as a result of the eye having a weak refracting force, or that the eye is too short from front to back or by a combination of both factors. In such an instance, in order for the rays to focus upon the retina, they must enter the eye in a coverging beam, and therefore a farsighted eye sees near objects worst of all. This type of eye is harder to correct but eyeglasses help it overcome the difficulty. Shooter's suffering from farsightedness will see the sights very poorly. The characteristic complaint of farsighted persons is that the rear notch seems to fuse with the front sight.

d. An indistinct, hazy image of objects on the retina can also result from astigmatism of the eye.

(1) An eye in which the refracting surfaces of the cornea and crystalline lens do not have a perfectly spherical form is called astigmatic. When an eye is astigmatic, parallel rays entering the eye cannot produce an exact focused image on the retina. The refraction of the light rays at various points in the eyeball occur at different angles. As a result, the eye possesses not a single principal focus, but several foci, which are located at various distances from the retina, that is why the image on it is indistinct and uneven (Figure 2-9). It must be said that certain strange phenomena frequently observed under practical conditions of marksmanship (for example, when two shooters are firing the same pistol, with an identical sight setting, and the centers of impact differ sharply from one another) are, in all probability, connected with astigmatism of the eye.

Figure 2-9. Scheme showing the Refraction of Rays in an Astigmatic Eye.

(2) One can easily be convinced of the existence or absence of astigmatism by making use of the chart on the following page (Figure 2-10). For this purpose it is necessary to look with one eye from the distance of best vision (approximately 10 feet) at a disk on which concentric circles are drawn If the person has astigmatism, only certain areas of the disk will be clearly visible and the remaining areas will seem hazy.

Figure 2-10. Chart for Discovering Astigmatism.

4. <u>Correction of Defects</u>: If even insignificant defects in vision are discovered, it is neces-sary to wear corrective eyeglasses when firing, since the excessive accommodation of the eye resulting from aiming will greatly fatigue vision and this can lead to a still greater decrease in its accuracy. It must also be kept in mind that when eyeglasses for firing are chosen by the ordinary method, that is, in an optometrist's office, the choice is not completely satisfactory for the shooter. It is very desirable when selecting the lenses to check them immediately on the pistol range, to make sure that one can see well the sight alignment located at arm's length distance away from the eye.   This selection is linked not so much with the determination of the lens dioptry, as with the determination of the quality of their grinding, since all defects will make themselves known quickly during such a check.

When wearing shooting glasses (including those with filter lenses) it is necessary to make sure that the line of sight runs perpendicular to the surface of the lens and through its center, since the central portion of the lens is usually ground considerably better and therefore has less distortion of the vision.   To hold the lenses perpendicular to the line of sight requires no change in the ordinary level placement of the head when assuming the firing position.

E. MONOCULAR AND BINOCULAR VISION.

It is necessary to dwell on one more peculiarity of our eyes which has tremendous importance in aiming--the existence of monocular and binocular vision.

1. <u>Vision with one eye is called monocular and vision with two is called binocular.</u> The fact that a person has two eyes does not always mean that he also has binocular vision. There are in-stances when the eye which has the poorest vision is not included in the act of vision and the person actually uses just one eye, the better one. The dominance of one eye over the other also occurs, even when both eyes possess identical sharpness of vision. The eye that the person prefers to use is called the dominant, or directing eye. There exists a very simple method by which one can determine which of the eyes is the stronger.

2. <u>In order to determine which is the dominant eye</u> the shooter must hold his hand out slightly making a ring out of the fingers and thumb, and look through it in such a way that some small object can be seen by both eyes (Figure 2-11.) Then, by alternately closing one eye then the other, it is necessary to see whether the object stays within the ring or leaves it. The dominant eye is the one with which the shooter sees the object as unshifted, remaining in the ring. In most people the dominant eye is the right one.

Figure 2-11. Determining which eye is dominant.

3. <u>The protracted work of one eye</u> (for example, by laboratory assistants, microscopists) contributes to the fact that the eye used becomes the dominant one. This naturally pertains also to shooters, who, when aiming, use one eye. The right eye is, in the overwhelming majority of cases, their dominant one.

4. <u>In the past the shooter has usually been instructed to squint his left eye</u> and aim the pistol at the target with his right eye. During subsequent instruction it is no longer necessary to continue this device of closing the eye, since it has its major shortcomings, which are attested to by numerous instance of medical research.

a. The first shortcoming is the strain which is involved in squinting the eye and is hard for most people to endure. Another undesirable aspect is the fact that the squinting of one eye is almost always accompanied by the tension and pressure of the closed lid on the eyeball. This pressure of the eyelid upon the eyeball affects the refraction of the crystaline lens and thus has an adverse influence upon the sharpness of vision of the open eye. The third factor having an adverse effect upon the accuracy of fire is the involuntary sympathetic dilation of the pupil of the open eye in response to the closing or squinting of the other eye. Thus, when excluding the second eye from work, it is best not to squint but suppress the visual impressions of the open left eye with an opaque disc which will allow equal light intensity to affect the eye.

b. With binocular aiming, that is, with both eyes open, the line of sight still is achieved with one eye. Consequently, this method does not involve anything new in principle and therefore the shooter is not required either to learn something new or to relearn something, but must simply stop closing one eye when aiming.

5. <u>Binocular aiming has a number of major advantages:</u> The shooter does not have to expend the additional effort involved in squinting the eye, and this is very important when he is engaged in prolonged firings. The binocular acuity of vision is usually better than the monocular. The visual perception of one eye intensifies the total stimulus sent to the central nervous system from the visual perception of the other eye. In such aiming, the stimuli sent by two eyes are more natural than those sent by a single one.

6. <u>All the movements of the eyeball,</u> as well as the holding of its fixed position at moments when the glance is fixed on some object, are effected by the work of three pairs of eye muscles. During the time when the eyes are at work, including the times when the eye is aiming, these muscles are in a state of indiscernible, slight vibration or quivering. For example, when aiming a pistol and the shooter turns his head down and to the right, the eyeball turns respectively upward and inward, it is held in the least desirable position; one that requires the combined, intensified work of all three groups of muscles (Figure 2-12). When the eye muscles become fatigued, the involuntary quivering of the eyeball increases considerably and this lessens the accuracy of aiming. Therefore, the shooter must devote major attention to the position of his head when firing. He must select that firing stance in which the head position is the most natural one, with the least amount of tilt, so that the shooter does not look at the target from under his eyebrows or sideways. This results in the rapid fatigue of the eye muscles and, hence, the lessening in the accuracy of aiming.

Figure 2-12. Muscles of the Right Eye. (Arrows Show the Direction in which the Eyeball turns when the Muscles designated by the numbers are contracted.

F. THE SHARPNESS OF VISION

The shooter is interested chiefly in the degree of the eye's differentiating sensitivity and its resultant sharpness of vision, as well as the degree of accuracy of aiming which the eye can guarantee.

1. <u>Basically, sharpness of vision depends upon the physical properties of the anatomy of the eye.</u> The physical condition of the eye determines primarily the greater or lesser accuracy of the image of the object upon the retina. These anatomical and physiological conditions determine how well we can see the object. The sharpness of the image upon the retina is the impression received by the brain.

2. <u>Sharpness of vision</u> is usually determined by the minimum space that we are able to see between two objects. In order for this space to be visible, it is necessary for at least one retinal element lying between the images of these two points to be stimulated. Thus, the normal sharpness of vision is generally considered to be that at which the eye can distinguish between two visible points at an angle of one minute.

3. <u>However, the anatomical dimensions of the retinal elements</u> (the rods and cones) do not completely determine the limit of visual acuity. Therefore, the visual acuity of the normal eye actually can be considerably greater than the medical norm. Research works have shown that the average visual acuity of the normal human eye, at one hundred yards under normal illumination, can distinguish distance between objects separated from one another within the limits of 40 angular minutes. This means that the normal eye can distinguish sufficiently clear, for example, a space of .1 inch between the side of the front sight and vertical inside surface of the rear sight notch on the pistol sight at a distance of one yard (the approximate distance to the muzzle and front sight). But the eye of an experienced shooter can distinguish a considerably smaller space between two objects. A number of experiments carried out by specialists attest to the greater accuracy of a trained shooter's sharpness of vision. For example, the vertical space between front and rear sight against a white background can be discerned down to the minute width of .01 inch.

4. <u>Many experiments confirm that the sharpness of vision can be considerably increased by means of exercises.</u> This increase in the sharpness of vision is achieved by searching for new signs new criteria for recognizing the form of objects. Such a sign for shooters is undoubtedly their highly-developed sense of symmetry and visual memory.

5. <u>Visual Memory:</u> Therefore, in order to achieve symmetry, a visual memory of correct sight alignment, with its symmetrical interrelationship of the front and rear sights, mainly, the equal amount of space between each side of the front and rear sights and the levelness of their horizontal surfaces, must be ingrained into the mind and never violated. No shot should be fired with less than perfection. All these factors, together with an existing sharpness of vision, will provide for accurate and consistent aiming and the accurate calling of the shot.

6. <u>Calling of the shot:</u> Accurate calling of a shot is dependent upon exact recall of the mental image of the sight alignment at the instant of firing. As demonstrated, the presence of 1/100th of an inch error in sight alignment will result in approximately a 3 inch error from target center at 50 yards. Acute awareness of the slightest degree of error in alignment is an absolute requirement of accurate shot calls from a clear visual memory. The overwhelming majority of shooters try to see the front sight sharply, and thus accept the blurring of the bull's eye. With the passage of time and with regular practice, the eye develops the ability to obtain the identical space relationship between the front sight and the rear sight and with increasing frequency can position the sights uniformly in the center of the aiming area which is blurred and out-of-focus.

Eventually, the shooter develops his visual powers to such an extent that the eye will consistently perform the act of aiming automatically and he can call his shots without error.

7. <u>Changing degrees of accuracy:</u> When the eye performs intensified work, not only the motor apparatus of the eye, but also its light-sensory apparatus has reduced efficiency. When the glance is fixed steadily upon some object, the eye possesses its greatest sharpness of vision for the first several seconds, after which the sharpness of the image on the retina, that is, the clear seeing of it, gradually decreases. Consequently, the shooter must not be captivated by excessively prolonged aiming, since, after the elaps of 12-16 seconds, his eye ceases to notice certain inaccuracies in aiming. By relying on the false assumption that the rear sight and front sight are in correct relationship to one another, the shooter makes grievous errors without noticing and therefore, does not know why they were committed.

129

a. If one calculates the time between the moment when the visual attention is concentrated on obtaining the precise alignment of the front and rear sights and the moment when the shooter makes the decision to positively press the trigger, the aiming process must not exceed 6-8 seconds.

b. When aiming, some shooters run their eye from the front sight to the rear sight notch and then to the third object, the target, doing this quickly several times, until these three points are all located on the same line. It must be said that his method of aiming causes rapid fatiguing of the muscular apparatus of the eye and fails to provide a constant objective for the formation of a visual memory. With this method of aiming it is very difficult for the shooter, for example, to conduct rapid fire, which is very limited in time. He simply does not have time to run his eye back and forth between objects located at varying distances. The shots may be fired when he is focused on any of the three objects. Consistently accurate shot calls are impossible. Therefore, when aiming, the shooter must strive to see only the front sight sharply and distinctly.

ANNEX III

PROCESSES OF THE HUMAN NERVOUS SYSTEM
RELEVANT TO EQUILIBRIUM, TRIGGER CONTROL AND HEARING

A. THE HUMAN NERVOUS SYSTEM CHARACTERISTICS

When any movement of the living organism is carried out, the nervous system necessarily takes part in the operation of any muscle. The stream of impulses coming from the central nervous system is the cause of the muscular contraction. The central nervous system determines the tone of the muscles, that is, their tense state, without which it would be impossible to cause movement or to keep the body in equilibrium in any position. Since a shooter must be very interested in the problem pertaining to muscular work directed at attaining trigger control and the achieving of the greatest immobility of the body when he assumes firing position, let us acquaint ourselves briefly in general outlines, with the arrangement of the human nervous system.

In all vertebrates, including man, distinction is made between the central nervous system and the peripheral nervous system.

1. The central nervous system represents a large accumulation of nerve tissue and consists of the spinal cord, situated within the spinal column, and the brain, situated within the cranial cavity.

2. The peripheral nervous system: The numerous nerves leading away from the spinal cord and the brain represent the peripheral nervous system. The principal property of the nerve tissue is that it conveys excitation.

a. The nerve consists of a large number of nerve fibers which are distinguished from one another chiefly by the thickness of the white covering. Not far from the place where it ends, the nerve fiber loses its white covering and breaks down into several small branches.

b. Thus, the nerves approaching the muscles consist of a large number of nerve endings. Within the muscle, each branches off sharply, providing with nerve ends an entire group of individual muscle fibers. The impulses from the ends of the centrifugal (see below) nerve fibers are transferred to the muscle fibers.

c. Smooth muscles, which are encountered chiefly within the walls of internal organs, possess comparatively weak excitability, contract very slowly. The cross-striped muscles conversely, are easily excited and the process of contraction in them occurs with great rapidity.

d. In accomplishing the work of immobile support of weapon and body, excitatory impulses coming from the central nervous system to the muscles always follow one another with great frequency, as a result of which the muscles do not have time to relax after each contraction. This leads to a fusing of separate contractions into one prolonged contraction. Such are the ordinary contractions of the skeletal muscles which we observe in the joints when there are extremely limited movements of the body and the muscles are kept in a state of immobility.

e. Excitatory impulses entering the muscles and causing them to contract are a response of the living organism to some irritation.

It is necessary to know that the nervous system carries out its work on the principle of the so-called reflex (reflex is a reflected action). Each action of an organism in response to an irritation coming from the outside or inside environment and occuring with the participation of the nervous system is called a reflex. The path taken by the excitatory impulses causing the reflex actions is called the reflex arc.

f. In any reflex arc it is possible to isolate a number of distinct areas.

(1) The first area of the reflex arc is made up of the receiving nerve ends -- the receivers -- which are situated in the sensory organs and in all other organs of the body -- the muscles, lungs, etc.

(2) The second is made up of the centripetal nerves carrying the excitation from the periphery (from the receiver) to the central nervous system.

131

Figure 3-10. Nerve Ends in a Skeletal Muscle.

(3) The third is made up of the central nervous system, where the excitation undergoes complex change.

(4) The fourth is the centrifugal nerve carrying the excitation from the central nervous system to a particular nerve or organ.

(5) The fifth is the termination of the centrifugal nerve in the organ giving the response action--the skeletal muscle, heart, glands, or smoother musculature.

g. Thus, all organs have received nerve ends, or receivers, which transmit the excitation to the central nervous system. Some receivers are situated within the body and receive stimuli arising in the internal organs; others are located near the surface of the body and receive external stimuli. As a result of the peculiarities of their structure, the receivers prove to be specialized, adapted to excitation only by definite stimuli; some receive stimuli from light, others from sound, etc. The specialized receivers also include muscular-motor receivers, which are excited by a change in the body's stance, thus contributing, in the final analysis, to maintaining it in equilibrium.

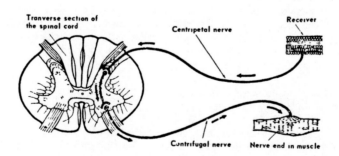

Figure 3-11. Diagram of a Reflector Arc.

132

B. NERVE PROCESSES IN EQUILIBRIUM CONTROL

1. <u>The affecting of a normal stance</u> of a living organism is provided for by the fact that the skeletal muscles are always somewhat in a state of tension. This phenomenon has been given the name of muscular tone. As a result of the existence of muscular tone, a definite interrelationship of various parts of the body of animals origan is maintained. The holding of the head and the body in normal position in space provides for the correct orientation of the organism with respect to the immediate environment and creates the necessary prerequisites for the organism's motor activity.

2. <u>Muscular tone is a reflex phonomenon.</u> The maintenance of the normal position of the body and of its equilibrium is provided for by a stream of impulses proceeding from the muscle and tendon receivers, the receivers of the skin, the vestibular apparatus and the retinas of the eyes, which impulses are transmitted along centripetal nerves to the central nervous system, causing a tonic-reflex activity of the skeletal muscles. In the process of gradual development, there arose and became fixed in the human organism a group of tonic reflexes aimed at maintaining equilibrium when there is a threat that it will be biolated or at restoring the normal stance in instances when the equilibrium had already been violated. This group of reactions was named the regulating tonic reflexes. They include: the posture reflexes, which arise when there is a change in the position of the head in space and with respect to the torso, and the straightening reflexes, which arise when the organism's normal position is altered. These reflexes lie in the redistribution of the tone of the muscles in the extremities, neck and torso. It is by this means that the skeletal musculature provides for the maintaining of equilibrium in the human body.

3. However, <u>as a result of the redistribution in the tension of the muscles</u> by means of the continuous action and counteraction of bending muscles and unbending muscles, the human body cannot be in a state of absolute equilibrium, cannot be completely immobile; it constantly shifts back and forth somewhat. Naturally, the shooter is interested in those conditions under which these shifts of the body under the action and counteraction of muscles are as small as possible.

a. Vestibular apparatus: (Equilibrium control)

In preserving the equilibrium of the body and, consequently, in the extent to which it shifts back and forth, great importance attaches to the impulses proceeding from the vestibular apparatus.

(1) The vestibular apparatus, the organ of equilibrium, is situated in the temporal portion of the head, in the inner portion of the right and left ear (Figure 12). It consists of the otolithic apparatus and the semicircle canals. The otolithic apparatus consists of two small pockets on the inner surface of which there are sensitive cells equipped with fine hairs. Small nodules of lime crystals-- otoliths--are located on the hairs. Any change in head position changes the tension on the hairs and thus excites the ends of nerve fibers, receivers, connected to the hairs. The tolerance for distinguishing between inclinations of the body to the side is 1º, and forward and back is 1.5-2º. The impulses coming from the otolithic apparatus cause reflex reactions contributing to maintaining the body in equilibrium. Three simicircular channels, which represent very fine tubes filled with a liquid--endolymph--lead away from one of the pockets of the otolithic apparatus in three planes perpendicular to one another. When the head makes a movement, the liquid contained in the channels, by moving back and forth, produces pressure upon the sensory cells connected to the ends of the nerve fibers. The impulses thus created cause reflex actions leading to the preservation of the body's equilibrium during movements.

(2) Consequently, when there is a change in the angle of the head or torso, there arises a number of reflexes directed at restoring their initial position. As soon as a person inclines his head, even if he does not change the position of his torso, impulses begin immediately to proceed from the vestibular apparatus. These impulses have an effect upon the change in muscle tone, that is, the tension of definite groups of muscles.

(3) It is completely natural that the vestibular apparatus will "work" with the greatest accuracy when the person's head is situated in its normal, natural position, without any inclination. The body of a shooter assuming firing position will undergo the least amount of shifting if his head is held in a normal position, without inclining it to either side. In this narrow tolerance of body inclination, the "sensitivity" of the vestibular apparatus, will be the greatest.

133

(4) The importance of the vestibular apparatus in providing for the stability of the stance when shooting is very great. The greater the extent to which the organ of equilibrium is developed and trained, the better its interrelation with the work of the skeletal musculature which is aimed at perserving the balance of the body.

b. The reflexes of stance equilibrium are carried out not only from the receivers of the vestibular apparatus, but also from the receivers in the muscles and tendons of the neck, and from the receivers in the skin in the neck area, which have been named the neck-tendon tonic reflexes of balance.

(1) From this the shooter must also make an appropriate conclusion for himself: When assuming a stance for shooting, it is not necessary to extend the head excessively toward the target, to throw the head back, that is not to strain the neck muscles and tendons excessively, since this causes strong stimulation of the receivers situated in them and thus creates a stream of impulses which lead to the redistribution of the tone of the skeletal musculature and to an increase in the number of times the body rocks, or moves back and forth.

(2) Finally, it is necessary to mention that the maintenance of muscular tone, and consequently the preservation of bodily equilibrium in a particular stance, is achieved by a stream of centripetal impulses, among which the impulses proceeding from the muscles and joints are of especial importance. The muscles are not only an organ of movement; thanks to the existence of special nerve ends which transmit impulses to the nervous system, the muscles simultaneously are also an organ which percieves the varying degree of their tensions and contractions. By constantly sending signals concerning the position of the body in space, the muscles and joints cause the corresponding reflex reactions, which lead to the preservation of the particular bodily balance. Therefore, when assuming firing stance the shooter must strive to achieve a position in which he does not exert too much tension on the powerful centripetal impulses which, so to speak, can drown out the weaker impulses proceeding from the other, less contracted muscles, and, in the final analysis, can have an over-all influence upon the redistribution of muscular tone, thus exerting an adverse effect upon the stability of the entire system consisting of the shooter's body and weapon.

C. NERVE PROCESSES IN TRIGGER CONTROL

As previously stated, all the movements of the human body are controlled by the nervous system. Under the influence of both external and internal stimuli, the nervous system enters a state of excitation. This excitation, arising at some center of stimulation, does not remain there, but extends along the corresponding nerve fibers, at a great rate of speed.

During shooting, the marksman has to execute various movements, each one of which is dictated by a set of external conditions. Ideally, each motion should be a condition reflex. For example, the visual perception of the minimum arc of movement in conjunction with perfect sight alignment should produce the conditioned reflex of applying positive pressure on the trigger. This desirable reaction of proper stimuli must be carried out rapidly.

1. Rapidity of Reaction: A reaction may be defined as the action taken by the individual in response to a certain stimulus. Despite the rapidity of one's reactions there is, nevertheless, an interval of time between the stimulus and the response. For example, there is a time lapse of between 0.18 and 0.25 seconds between the time the shooter perceives the need for trigger action, as induced by the visual stimulus of correct sight alignment and minimum arc of movement and the moment he initiates trigger control. This reaction time is determined in part by the fact that it takes a certain amount of time for the image formed by the correct sight alighment and minimum arc of movement to be transmitted through the retina to the brain, from which the decision to put the trigger finger into motion must come.

The shooter must know that the speed of reaction is directly dependent upon the mobility of the nervous processes of stimulation and inhibition. The more rapidly the nerve cells of the corresponding areas of the central nervous system change over from the state of inhibition to the state of stimulation, the more rapid the reaction.

2. Excitation-Stimulation and Inhibition: The coordination of aiming and applying pressure to the trigger requires the shooter to be decisive in his actions. If his reaction time is too slow, his actions in response to visual perceptions will be delayed and will lose their efficiency. In this case, the

134

shot would not be delivered under the optimum conditions, and the resulting hit on the target would suffer accordingly. The question naturally arises, then, of whether or not the shooter's reactions are fast enough, or whether or not they always remain the same. The answer is quite simple. The shooter's reactions are not fast enough, and they do not always remain the same. The explanation is also simple. In addition to the process of excitation, which has just been described, there exists also a process which is labelled inhibition. It has been demonstrated by scientists, that this phenomenon arises in the central nervous system in conjunction with the process of stimulation. Moreover, their actions are simultaneous. The state of inhibition must not be considered a state of rest or inactivity; it represents an active state of the nerve cells in which stimulation cannot pass through them. The simultaneous existence of the process of stimulation and inhibition is the only thing that permits the living organism to execute various movements. For example, in order to bend the index finger and thus produce the action of pressing on the trigger, it is necessary for the stimulating impulses to contract the finger flexors. If only the process of stimulation existed, the coordinated activity of the organism and all kinds of movements executed by it, would be impossible, since the process of stimulation in this instance would extend not only to the flexors, but also to the extensors. It would be completely impossible, without this joint work of antagonist muscles, to bend the finger or perform any other similar movement.

3. The shooter's rapidity of reaction is influenced primarily by the degree of his experience, when, as a result of training, the perfection of the shooter's movements is achieved chiefly by means of improving the work of the nervous system. In order to analyze those complex phenomena which occur when the shooter is mastering the meter habits necessary to execute the coordinated action of aiming and pressing the trigger, let us turn to a theory of higher nervous activity.

a. When the shooter is just beginning to train himself in the correct control of the trigger action, the muscular activity at first causes a predominance of the process of stimulation in the cerebral cortex. During the initial phase of training, the process of stimulation spreads within the cerebral cortex area of the brain encompassing considerable areas of it. The process of stimulation arising at one place in the motor area spreads over a considerable area of the cortex, leading to a situation in which muscular groups which do not take direct participation in an action are drawn into it. Properly speaking, this is a definite reason why beginners, instead of pressing on the trigger by merely moving the trigger finger, accompany its movement by the work of many groups of arm and hand muscles, thus spoiling the aim of the pistol at the most critical moment of producing the shot.

b. Subsequently, as the shooter practices and his habits become ingrained, he learns to limit excesssive moments. Soon afterwards he is able to develop a certain restraint of movements. Because the shooter, by means of concentrated practice, has intensified the process of inhibition, the widespread predominance of stimulation in the cerebral cortex is followed by a restriction of stimulation to limited areas. Frequently, during this period of training, the shooter notices that he does not always press the trigger at exactly the right moment. Many shooters are aware of the rather unpleasant sensation that arises from the many times that the trigger seems to come to a complete stop, and refuses to fire the pistol. Many a shooter has been heard to wail "the trigger just stays there, the finger won't mash." After an interval, the pistol begins to describe an enlarged arc of movement, and the shooter, even as he realizes that the best moment for producing the shot has been lost, continues pressure on the triggers with the usual disastrous results. Subsequently, after systematic training, the shooter improves further the interactions between the process of stimulation and inhibition, and as a result, his movements and timing improve, and are accompanied by the coordinated work of only the necessary groups of muscles.

4. Developing Coordination: As he masters and strengthens his motor habits, the shooter soon acquires conditioned reactions that allow him to perform precisely certain movements. He then must learn to coordinate these various actions into the timely and smooth movement of the trigger finger. These actions are specifically the acquisition of correct sight alignment and attaining a minimum arc of movement.

a. It must be said that even highly trained shooters who as a result of prolonged training have achieved the strengthening of the corresponding work habits and the automation of the movement in controlling the trigger action, are unable, under certain circumstances, to maintain the equilibrium of the process of stimulation and inhibition. This, naturally, has an effect upon the seed of reaction and the coordination of the movement. For example, when changing over from prolonged rest to the start of action, the organism is not drawn immediately into the work. Shortly after waking up, a shooters performance will, as a rule, not be as good as it will be later, since the process of inhibition will predominate in the interactions between the process of stimulation and inhibition. As a result the reaction will prove to be delayed and the movements will not be sufficiently prompt or accurate.

b. The shooters speed of reaction and the coordination of his movements are greatly influenced by: the duration of the interval between periods of training; preliminary stretching and limbering up to promote alertness before each firing; and the shooter's mood and emotional state (emotions are psychological processes involved in the experiencing of satisfaction and dissatisfaction), especially under competitive conditions.

c. It follows from all this that the difficulties confronting the shooter when controlling the trigger action lie primarily in the fact that the shooter's speed of reaction to the external stimulus (the aligned front and rear sights coinciding with the minimum arc of movement) is inconstant and depends upon the degree of balance between the processes of stimulation and inhibition. It is the factor in the final analysis, which determines the rapidity and coordination of the shooter's movements.

5. Reflexes: However, there are difficulties of another nature which the shooter encounters when pressing the trigger and producing a shot. These difficulties evolve from the fact that the shot itself is accompanied by loud sound and the recoil of the pistol; these difficulties are linked with the necessity of changing the process of certain reflex reactions in the organism of the shooter.

As is well known all actions performed by a person proceed according to the type of reflexes (a reflex is the organism's reaction, carried out with the participation of the central nervous system, in response to a stimulus). Depending upon the peculiarities of the reactions, all reflexes of the living organism are divided into two classes:

a. Unconditioned reflexes: Unconditioned reflexes are innate, constant reaction of the organism in response to definite external stimuli. They do not have to be developed specially and they always manifest themselves under strictly definite conditions. However, despite the fact that unconditioned reflexes are innate, in case of necessity the cerebral cortex can influence them and change their course.

b. Conditioned reflexes: Conditioned reflexes are temporary reactions of the organism which are individually acquired during the life of the organism. They are developed under the action of the immediate environment, and depend upon many conditions. Conditioned reflexes are always carried out with the participation of the cerebral cortex. During the course of a person's life, he constantly encounters the external world. In order to live, he must adapt, react to the influence of the environment and make it over in the direction that he requires. This link between the organism and the external environment, is realized partially by simple, unconditioned reflexes, but chiefly by means of creating new conditioned reflexes.

(1) Conditioned reflexes which have been developed can be retained for a long time only in the event that they are reinforced, at least now and then by corresponding stimuli. Consequently, conditioned reflexes are temporary. From this it follows that conditioned reflexes are inhibited comparatively easily and disappear when the necessity for them no longer exists.

(2) The conditioned reflex situation becomes considerably more complicated when accompanied by a change in innate, unconditioned reflexes. It is precisely these unconditioned reflexes which marksmanship requires a person to change, especially when he is learning to control the trigger action and produce the shot.

c. It is in this light that we shall attempt to analyze some of the reflex reactions occuring in the shooter's organism in response to the external stimulus--first, the shot, accompanied by a strong auditory effect, and then the recoil of the pistol.

(1) Prevent development of detrimental conditioned reflexes: Everyone knows that a person reacts to an unexpected sharp sound--a shot, cry, etc. --by an involuntary sharp flinch, which is an unconditioned reflex to the auditory stimulus. Naturally, if the shooter reacts in that way to his own shot or to that of his neighbor on the firing line, it will be impossible to have accurate shooting. Therefore, the shooter must train himself to remain indifferent to such external stimuli and thus to muffle the innate, unconditioned reflex.

(2) If someone waves something threateningly at another person, or say, claps his hands in front of his face or fires a shot unexpectedly, the person will involuntarily, unconsciously

136

close his eyes, that is, blink. This reaction of the person is a manifestation of an innate, unconditioned defensive reflex. However, despite this fact, shooting requires a person, during aiming and firing (his own or that of neighbor) to keep his eyes open, otherwise his aiming will be inaccurate and, in addition, he will not be able to call the shot, that is, establish the interrelation of the centered front sight and the rear-sight notch at the moment of fire. Consequently, the shooter must learn to suppress this defensive unconditioned reflex.

(3) To each action causing pain, a person responds with an involuntary sharp movement accompanied by a contraction of muscular groups. This represents an unconditioned reflex. Now let us imagine that a beginner who previously has never fired a pistol has gone out onto the firing line. If he is given practice cartridges, he will calmly load the pistol with them, aim and press the trigger. But as soon as he produces one or two shots with a live cartridge and feels the blow in the hand from the recoil, which, in addition, is accompanied by an auditory effect, he will subsequently act completely different. Knowing that the shot is accompanied by a blow in the hand, the beginner, in addition to pressing the trigger, will involuntarily strain his muscles, stiffen his arm and press his shoulder forward in order to counteract the expected blow. Thus, a conditioned reflex to the expected blow has already appeared on the base of the beginner's unconditioned reflex. If steps are not taken in time, this conditioned reflex which has manifested itself will become stronger and become a harmful habit for the shooter. Consequently, the shooter must learn not only to suppress certain unconditioned reflexes, but also to prevent the development and reinforcement of conditioned reflexes which are detrimental to shooting--this instance, the expectation of the blow from the pistol recoil -- and when the blow itself occurs, to learn how to keep unchanged the pose of the body and the degree of muscular tension, so as not to spoil the aim.

As we can see, the process of the coordinated action of the timely pressure on the trigger and correct aiming under the conditions of a shot accompanied by recoil and an auditory effect makes very great demands upon the person's nervous system. The necessity of achieving equilibrium in the process of stimulation and inhibition, the necessity of suppressing certain innate, unconditioned reflexes which are detrimental to shooting create very great difficulties which are not so simple for the shooter to overcome.

D. THE PREVENTION OF DAMAGE TO THE SHOOTER'S HEARING

1. General: Repeated exposure to loud noise leads to deafness. What is less well known is that it is possible to prevent deafness caused by loud noise. The methods to prevent the damage to shooter's hearing are relatively simple. Further, the use of these methods need not cause discomfort that would interfere with performance during competitive shooting. Army Regulation 40-5 makes it mandatory that ear protection be utilized during the exposure of personnel to ear-damaging noise.

2. The Danger to Hearing:

a. The human ear is a very delicate organ which can adapt and function efficiently over a wide range of noise levels. In a still forest an undamaged human ear can detect the near-silent movement of birds and small animals. Against the background of noise in a roaring factory, the same ear can discriminate and register the sound of human voice. Usually, the ear can serve alternatively in both circumstances if given time to adapt. However, like any delicate piece of equipment, there is a limit to the punishment the ear can endure without damage. The constant bludgeoning of the auditory nerves by the explosions of small arms in close proximity is more than the human hearing apparatus can tolerate without damage.

b. Persons, vary in their susceptibility to ear damage caused by loud noise. Some persons' ears are quite sensitive and after shooting only a few rounds these personnel will have continuous "tinnitus" (ringing in the ears). They may experience a hearing loss, i.e., partial deafness. Other persons seem to be able to shoot indefinitely with only fleeting tinnitus and the minimal hearing loss, as measured by the audiometers. The latter type of personnel are in the very rare minority. Audiometer testing of light weapons instructors at Fort Jackson, South Carolina (1963) determined that over half had hearing loss so extensive that they received physical profiles of H-3 or worse. Only about twenty percent of these instructor-shooters could be retained on active duty by waiver of this physical disability.

c. Noise intensity is measured in decibels (db). The human ear is uniformly damaged by noise of steady intensity over 90 db and by instantaneous pulses of noise over 140 db. Small arms firing causes instantaneous noise over 160 db. (This is about 100 times as intense as 140 db, since the decibel system of measuring noise intensity is a logarithmic scale). It is not surprising that a shooter's hearing can become severely impaired if proper protection is not utilized. This deafness and the often associated permanent tinnitus are preventable.

3. The United States Army Hearing Conservation Program: While the Army's program of hearing conservation is medical in its inception and supervision, the execution of the prevention of hearing loss is a command function. From the shooter's stand-point, there is one prevalent noise hazard - the explosions of small arms ammunition. The Hearing Conservation Program for shooters and marksmanship instructors consists of regular audiometer and physical examination of hearing and ears of these noise-exposed personnel, combined with preventive measures established at the firing range. The latter consist of engineering controls of hazardous noise by sound insulation, noise baffles, and other means to reduce and muffle the noise and its echos. This is combined with personnel protective devices.

4. Personnel Hearing Protective Devices.

a. Personnel protective devices are as far as shooters are concerned, either fitted ear plugs or ear muffs. Ear plugs are small, inexpensive and easy to carry. They come in five (5) sizes. They are made of soft plastic and adjust to fit any ear. Ear plugs are a medical supply item and available through any dispensory or military hospital. Ear muffs are obviously more cumbersome and expensive but are more comfortable and effective in attenuating high decibel sound. Ear muffs do a better job of ear protection than do the ear plugs. The ear muffs are available through non-medical supply channels.

b. The following are acceptable U.S. Army issue hearing protective devices:

EAR PLUGS

FSN	NOMENCLATURE	UNIT
6515-664-7858	PLUG, Ear, Noise Protection, Extra Small, 24s:	pkg
6515-299-8290	PLUG, Ear, Noise Protection, Small, 24s:	pkg
6515-299-8289	PLUG, Ear, Noise Protection, Medium, 24s:	pkg
6515-299-8288	PLUG, Ear, Noise Protection, Large, 24s:	pkg
6515-664-7859	PLUG, Ear, Noise Protection, Extra Large, 24s:	pkg
6515-082-2675	PLUG, Ear, Noise Protection, Regular, Triple Flange, 24s: (Plastic Sterilizable)	pkg
6515-082-2676	PLUG, Ear, Noise Protection, Small, Triple Flange, 24s: (Plastic Sterilizable)	pkg
6515-299-8287	CASE, Ear Plug, Plastic, 12s; (This Case holds one pair of any of the above mentioned plugs)	pkg
6530-889-9026	BOTTLE, Snap-on Cap, Plastic, 72s (The cost of this item is much less than that of the standard ear plug case)	pkg

EAR MUFFS

FSN	NOMENCLATURE	UNIT
4240-226-6016	AURAL Protector, Sound, High Performance, M1200: (mfg: American Optical Co.)	ea
4240-464-0253	AURAL Protector, Sound High Performance, M8A: (mfg: David Clark Co.)	ea
4240-856-6650	AURAL Protector, Sound, High Performance, M19A: (mfg: David Clark Co.)	ea
4240-861-3612	AURAL Protector, Sound, High Performance, (mfg: Mine Safety Appliances Co.)	ea
4240-991-1910	AURAL Protector, Sound, High Performance, M258 (mfg: Willson Co.)	ea

c. It is an absolute requirement that unit commanders and other responsible persons enforce the use of either ear muffs or ear plugs by all personnel who may be shooting or those instructors and coaches who function in a position on the firing line.

Appendix to Annex III - Processes Of the Human Nervous System
Relevant to Equilibrium, Hearing and Trigger and Control

OCCUPATIONAL HEALTH

Extract   (AR 40-5)
5-1

5-1. General. The specific objectives of the occupational health program of the Army are to:

    a. Assure that all eligible personnel (military and civilian) are physically, mentally, and psychologically suited to their work, and that their physical and mental health and well-being are maintained during service or employment.

    b. Determine that the work environment for noncombatant areas is safe, hygienic, and wholesome.

    c. Reduce the economic loss occasioned by physical inefficiency, sickness, and injury of military personnel and civilian employees.

*   *   *   *   *   *   *   *   *   *   *   *   *   *   *   *   *   *   *   *

5-5. Hearing conservation program

    a. General. This paragraph establishes minimum standards for the control of overexposure to potentially hazardous noise of a steady-state or impulse type from firing small arms or munitions; transportation, power, or other mechanical sources; and other industrial or military activities.

    b. Engineering control of hazardous noise: Whenever operations permit, exposures to potentially hazardous noise will be eliminated or reduced to the maximum extent possible by engineering or operational controls.

    c. Personal protection devices: Whenever it is not possible by engineering methods to reduce noise to safe levels, or workers cannot be excluded from noisy areas, personnel protective devices to attenuate the ambient noise in the ear canal are required. These devices are of four types: ear plugs (pre-formed or malleable) that fit into the ear canal; ear muffs, that fit over the external ear; helmets equipped with sound reducing ear pieces; and semi-inserts that fit into the ear canal but are supported by head-set type bands. Helmets and semi-inserts may be integral portions of communication equipment. Ordinarily where electronic communication systems are not involved, ear plugs and ear muffs are used, either singularly or in combination.

    (1) Commanders will insure that this equipment will be worn whenever personnel are exposed to potentially hazardous noise levels. These are no simple field criteria for judging accurately the degree of hazard from noise. A complete survey of the noise, including an octave band analysis and consideration of time of exposure, is essential to any definitive determination of whether a steady-state noise exposure is hazardous to the hearing of personnel. For field guidance, those noise levels considered potentially hazardous are 90 decibels overall level for steady-state noise, an instantaneous peak value in excess of 140 decibels for impulse noise, or as specified by the surgeon when qualified medical personnel and equipment for making and interpreting noise surveys are available. Requests for assistance will be referred to The Surgeon General, ATTN: MEDPS-PO.

    (2) Commanders will insure that a combination of ear plugs and ear muffs will be worn when exposures are necessary to noise intensities of 120 db, or more, of steady-state noise, if electronic communication systems are not involved. In this regard, it is being assumed that ear plugs or ear muffs alone provide 30 decibels of protection against noise, and that combined these devices provide a total of 40 decibels of attenuation. It should be recognized, however, that because of possible poor fit of ear plugs or ear muffs, the 30 decibels of singular or 40 decibels of combined attenuation may not be achieved.

140

(3) Commanders will designate the specific areas where the wearing of ear protective devices is required and will provide instructions in the proper use of available ear protection devices

(4) Personnel provided ear protective devices will properly use and conserve such equipment and exercise due care in keeping this equipment in a sanitary condition.

(5) Personal protective devices will be purchased within current budgetary resources.

*   *   *   *   *   *   *   *   *   *   *   *   *   *   *   *   *   ⁖

ANNEX IV

PROBLEMS OF WOMEN PISTOL SHOOTERS

The field of competitive pistol shooting is open to women. The United States needs more women pistol competitors in both National and International competition. Starting with the 1971 Pan-American Games, women's events will be standard in International competition. Women may now compete in the World and Olympic Games.

A. SCOPE.

The fundamentals of pistol shooting are the same for both men and women. This annex will discuss the thoughts and actions necessary for the female marksman to shoot a ten and will cover some of the problems in competitive shooting that are peculiar to women. We will review the shooting equipment and how variations of this equipment will help to improve scores; the differences in the physique of women that demand development of greater muscular strength to hold the weapon firm and steady; proper clothing necessary to be comfortable on the firing line and the responsibilities of women in the field of home firearms safety.

B. EQUIPMENT AND WEAPONS.

Having the proper equipment is necessary to winning scores. As shooters, you must determine the type of equipment best for you. When you are attending a pistol match, observe the different types of weapons being fired on the line and note the comparative results. Later, inquire at your local club to see if some of the members have the different types of weapons which you could possibly fire. Get a cross section of opinion as to their merits and deficiencies. If you borrow a weapon to fire, remember to give it the best of care and treatment. Return it to the owner in the same condition as you received it. If it is dirty, clean it before returning. Decide for yourself if the pistol is suitable for you. People with small hands will find the revolver more difficult to operate than the semi-automatic.

In firing the caliber .45 pistol or the caliber .38 pistol built on a .45 frame, you may find the stock too large for your hand. If your hand is very small, use the Model 1911 flat mainspring housing rather than the raised mainspring housing of the Model 1911A1 caliber .45 pistol.

If you find it difficult to control the recoil of the large caliber pistols consider a barrel rib for additional weight and custom grips. The inertia of additional weight slows down gun movement and custom grips will allow you to get a firm grip each time you fire.

Your shooting box should be large enough to hold all shooting accessories yet small and light enough for you to carry without undue strain. Check all available pistol boxes and decide on the one that suits your needs. A carrier similar to a golf bag cart is a great help in moving a gun box to the firing line.

D. PHYSICAL FITNESS.

1. In order to use your shooting equipment effectively, you must be physically fit. There are several areas that generally need improvement. Increasing the strength of the shooting arm, shoulder, torso and leg muscles will help in holding the weapon steady and provide the stamina needed to shoot a 2700 aggregate in one day.

2. The Candidan 5BX Plan and Cooper's AEROBICS are two good sources for you to plan a long term physical program. Once you have a plan stick to it!

3. One of the problems women experience is the shortening of the heel tendons caused by wearing high heels for long periods of time. Exercise is needed to add strength and length to the heel tendon. Wear flat heels as much as possible.

D. CLOTHING.

You now have the necessary equipment and a program for physical conditioning. This preparation is wasted if you go to the line wearing a tight skirt and tall hairdo. Proper clothing is essential. Your shoes should give support to the feet and have flat contact with the ground. If you have weak ankles, wear boots that give additional support. Loose fitting slacks, burmuda shorts, or a skirt that has a pocket in which to place your non-shooting hand while shooting will prove practical on the firing line. Your blouse should not bind the shoulders and should give free movement. Think about protection for your arms from hot brass, sunburn and chill in cool weather. If your blouse has short sleeves, make arrangements for something to cover your arms. Also, be sure it is closed at the neck while firing. Hot brass down the neck is very disconcerting. You should wear a hat to protect you from the sun, rain, and hot brass.

E. FIREARMS SAFETY IN THE FAMILY.

A problem closely related to women shooters is the responsibility to the whole family in regard to firearms safety.

What can you do as a homemaker and mother to insure the safety of your family in handling of weapons and ammunition?

1. Plan an individual program tailored to fit your family. Include the following:

a. Detailed instruction to all children on the correct way to handle weapons and ammunition.

b. Time spent with the children to insure they know and understand the dangers associated with weapons and ammunition.

c. Children must not handle weapons unless there is adult supervision.

d. Keep all weapons in the home under lock and key.

e. All ammunition should be stored in a locked place away from the weapons.

f. Write to the NRA for specific rules to include in a home safety course for your family.

2. Remember, guns don't kill people, people kill people.

F. SUMMARY.

There is room in competitive shooting for women. Most of the fundamentals are the same for both men and women. We have discussed some of the problems peculiar to women and how to overcome them. You must develop your muscular system to improve your ability to hold the weapon firm and steady. Your clothes must fit you and the weather conditions. You can add to home safety by giving instructions to your family on firearms safety.

GLOSSARY OF TERMS

ASSEMBLY AREA is a designated zone in the rear of the firing line, approximately 25 yards, where the next relay of competitors can complete their preparations for the match and receive instruction and advice from their coach or team captain.

AIMING AREA is the center area of the target as against an aiming point on the target which is extremely difficult to attain due to the universal presence of movement in the shooter's hold.

BREATH CONTROL is the ability to temporarily suspend breathing while firing a shot without being conscious of the need to take another breath. This awareness disturbs the shooter's concentration on maintaining perfect sight alignment.

BALL AND DUMMY is a training exercise wherein the shooter makes an effort to employ all the control factors for firing a good shot. The ammunition inserted into the pistol by the coach is a random selection of live or dummy ammunition. This training aids the shooter in overcoming reaction to the recoil and loud noise of firing, preventing uncontrolled reflexes from disturbing the hold, and perfecting sight alignment.

THE CENTER FIRE PISTOL FOR INTERNATIONAL COMPETITION is similar to the pistol used in NRA domestic competition. The trigger pull is three pounds as compared to the NRA requirement of 2 1/2 pounds. Caliber .38 is the normal size used.

DRY FIRING is a training exercise wherein the shooter employs all the factors of controlling the firing of an accurate shot without using live ammunition.

FOLLOW THROUGH is the effort on the part of the shooter to continue the employment of the fundamentals throughout the deliver of the shot exactly as they were planned and set-up.

THE FREE PISTOL is a special design of competitive weapon for achieving the ultimate in accuracy from a handgun. It is 22 caliber long rifle. The majority of free pistols have a longer barrel than the normal pistol and an extended sight radius. The trigger weight is extremely light and is adjustable from 1/2 oz to 1 1/2 ozs. There is a form fitting grip for the hand.

THE FUNDAMENTALS OF PISTOL MARKSMANSHIP are those essential factors that the shooter must know and learn to control in order to fire an accurate shot.

THE GRIP of the shooting hand on the pistol provides the shooter with a firm hold on the weapon that prevents shifting during recoil and a natural alignment of the sights without moving the head or wrist from their normal attitudes.

HARD BALL ammunition is the term used to describe the .45 caliber service type of pistol ammunition.

INTERNATIONAL SHOOTING UNION is the organizaion that sponsors and controls all international firing competitions between nations. The headquarters is in Weisbaden, West Germany.

MENTAL DISCIPLINE in pistol marksmanship is the shooter's ability to maintain his concentration on sight alignment while the other fundamentals of minimum arc of movement and trigger control are being employed at their optimum.

MINIMUM ARC OF MOVEMENT is the smallest degree of movement that the shooter can attain in the body, shooting arm and weapon during the time of firing a shot.

THE NATIONAL MATCH COURSE OF FIRE is a three stage pistol match. The first stage is ten shots in ten minutes, fired at 50 yards. The second stage is two strings of five shots each timed fire, 20 seconds each string at 25 yards. The third stage is two strings of five shots each rapid fire, ten seconds each string at 25 yards for a total of 30 shots.

POSITIVE PRESSURE on the trigger is an uninterrupted, constantly increasing pressure applied by the trigger finger in an effort to fire the shot. This pressure is initiated by the presence of a satisfactory minimum arc of movement in conjunction with perfect sight alignment, not perfect sight picture. A perfect sight picture is the absence of movement combined with perfect sight alignment.

POSITION of a pistol shooter is the relationship of the shooter's body to the target. Proper or natural positioning of the shooter's body points the shooting arm directly at the target center without deviation

RAPID FIRE is a type of pistol match or a stage of the National Match Course of fire where a string of five shots are fired consecutively during a period of ten seconds. A Rapid Fire Match is a series of four such strings and the National Match Course includes two strings.

THE RAPID FIRE PISTOL is a special design of competitive 22 caliber short weapon for firing in international rapid fire competition. It's outstanding characteristics are minimum recoil, dependability and fast semi-automatic operation.

SQUADDING TICKET is a card issued to each shooter in a pistol match that indicates the caliber of weapon, the relay of firing, and the target number for each of a succession of matches scheduled to be fired during the tournament.

SLOW FIRE is a type of pistol match or a stage of the National Match Course of fire where a period of one minute is allowed for each of a maximum of 10 or 20 shots.

SIGHT ALIGNMENT is the relationship of the front sight to the notch of the rear sight as seen by the shooter's eye. The top of the front sight must be level with the top of the rear sight and the light space must be equal on each side for the front sight.

STANCE is the posture assumed by a pistol shooter while firing a shot.

THE INTERNATIONAL STANDARD PISTOL is similar to the caliber .22 weapons used in domestic NRA competition. The barrel length is limited to 15 centermeters and the trigger pull is limited to 1000 grams.

TIMED FIRE is a type of pistol match or a stage of the national match course of fire where a string of five shots are fired consecutively during a period of 20 seconds. A timed fire match is a series of four such strings and the National Match Course includes two strings.

TRIGGER CONTROL is the ability of the pistol shooter to apply pressure on the trigger to fire the weapon without disturbing sight alingment.

WAD - CUTTER pistol ammunition has a type of bullet that is shaped to cut a clean hole in the target face. This sharp edge enables the scorer to readily and accurately evaluate the hit.

ZEROING is the technique of setting your sights so that a shot called good, (undisturbed perfect sight alignment and minimum arc of movement) will hit the center of the target on an ideal day with no wind.

Printed in the United States
45373LVS00006B/103

9 781589 636316